HONOR

Oh, I may give it up: he's full of his new boots—and singing, see!

[Enter **PHIL McBRIDE**, dressed in the height of the Irish buck-farmer fashion, singing,

"Oh the boy of Ball'navogue!
Oh the dasher! oh the rogue!
He's the thing! and he's the pride
Of town and country, Phil McBride—
All the talk of shoe and brogue!
Oh the boy of Ball'navogue!"

There's a song to the praise and glory of your—of your brother, Honor! And who made it, do you think, girl?

HONOR

Miss Caroline Flaherty, no doubt. But, dear Phil, I've a favour to ask of you.

PHIL

And welcome! What? But first, see! isn't there an elegant pair of boots, that fits a leg like wax?—There's what'll plase Car'line Flaherty, I'll engage. But what ails you, Honor?—you look as if your own heart was like to break. Are not you for the fair to-day?—and why not?

HONOR

Oh! rasons.
[Aside]
Now I can't speak.

PHIL

Speak on, for I'm dumb and all ear—speak up, dear—no fear of the father's coming out, for he's leaving his bird (*i.e. beard*) in the bason, and that's a work of time with him.—Tell all to your own Phil.

HONOR

Why then I won't go to the fair—because—better keep myself to myself, out of the way of meeting them that mightn't be too plasing to my father.

PHIL

And might be too plasing to somebody else—Honor McBride.

HONOR

Oh, Phil, dear! But only promise me, brother, dearest, if you would this day meet any of the Rooneys—

PHIL

That means Randal Rooney.

HONOR

No, it was his mother Catty was in my head.

PHIL

A bitterer scould never was!—nor a bigger lawyer in petticoats, which is an abomination.

HONOR

'Tis not pritty, I grant; but her heart's good, if her temper would give it fair play. But will you promise me, Phil, whatever she says—you won't let her provoke you this day.

PHIL

How in the name of wonder will I hinder her to give me provocation? and when the spirit of the McBrides is up—

HONOR

But don't lift a hand.

PHIL

Against a woman?—no fear—not a finger against a woman.

HONOR

But I say not against any Rooney, man or woman. Oh, Phil! dear, don't let there be any fighting betwixt the McBride and Rooney factions.

PHIL

And how could I hinder if I would? The boys will be having a row, especially when they get the spirits— and all the better.

HONOR

To be drinking! Oh! Phil, the mischief that drinking does!

PHIL

Mischief! Quite and clane the contrary—when the shillelah's up, the pike's down. 'Tis when there'd be no fights at fairs, and all sober, then there's rason to dread mischief. No man, Honor, dare be letting the whiskey into his head, was there any mischief in his heart.

HONOR

Well, Phil, you've made it out now cliverly. So there's most danger of mischief when men's sober—is that it?

PHIL

Irishmen?—ay; for sobriety is not the nat'ral state of the craturs; and what's not nat'ral is hypocritical, and a hypocrite is, and was, and ever will be my contempt.

HONOR

And mine too. But—

PHIL

But here's my hand for you, Honor.
They call me a beau and a buck, a slasher and dasher, and flourishing Phil.

Love and Law by Maria Edgeworth

A DRAMA. IN THREE ACTS.

Maria Edgeworth was born at Black Bourton, Oxfordshire on January 1st 1768. Her early years were with her mother's family in England. Sadly, her mother died when Maria was five.

Maria was educated at Mrs Lattafière's school in Derby in 1775. There she studied dancing, French and other subjects. Maria transferred to Mrs Devis's school in Upper Wimpole Street, London. Her father began to focus more attention on Maria in 1781 when she nearly lost her sight to an eye infection.

She returned home to Ireland at 14 and took charge of her younger siblings. She herself was home-tutored by her father in Irish economics and politics, science, literature and law. Despite her youth literature was in her blood. Maria also became her father's assistant in managing the family's large Edgeworthstown estate.

Maria first published 1795 with 'Letters for Literary Ladies'. That same year 'An Essay on the Noble Science of Self-Justification', written for a female audience, advised women on how to obtain better rights in general and specifically from their husbands.

'Practical Education' (1798) is a progressive work on education. Maria's ambition was to create an independent thinker who understands the consequences of his or her actions.

Her first novel, 'Castle Rackrent' was published anonymously in 1800 without her father's knowledge. It was an immediate success and firmly established Maria's appeal to the public.

Her father married four times and the last of these to Frances, a year younger and a confidante of Maria, who pushed them to travel more widely: London, Britain and Europe were all now visited.

The second series of 'Tales of Fashionable Life' (1812) did so well that she was now the most commercially successful novelist of her age.

She particularly worked hard to improve the living standards of the poor in Edgeworthstown and to provide schools for the local children of all and any denomination.

After a visit to see her relations Maria had severe chest pains and died suddenly of a heart attack in Edgeworthstown on 22nd May 1849. She was 81.

Index of Contents

DRAMATIS PERSONÆ

MEN

MR CARVER, of Bob's Fort. A Justice of the Peace in Ireland.

OLD MATTHEW McBRIDE. A rich Farmer.

PHILIP McBRIDE. His Son.

RANDAL ROONEY. Son of the Widow Catherine Rooney and a Lover of Honor McBride.

MR GERALD O'BLANEY. A Distiller

PATRICK COXE. Clerk to Gerald O'Blaney.

WOMEN

MRS CARVER. Wife of Mr. Carver.

MISS BLOOMSBURY. A fine London Waiting-maid of Mrs. Carver's.

MRS CATHERINE ROONEY, commonly called CATTY ROONEY. A Widow—Mother of Randal Rooney.

HONOR McBRIDE. Daughter of Matthew McBride, and Sister of Philip McBride.

A Justice's Clerk—a Constable—Witnesses—and two Footmen.

LOVE AND LAW

ACT I

SCENE I

A Cottage.—A Table—Breakfast.

HONOR McBRIDE, alone.

HONOR
Phil!—
[Calls]
—Phil, dear! come out.

PHIL [Answers from within]
Wait till I draw on my boots!

All that I am, may be; but there's one thing I am not, and will never be—and that's a bad brother to you. So you have my honour, and here's my oath to the back of it. By all the pride of man and all the consate of woman—where will you find a bigger oath?—happen what will, this day, I'll not lift my hand against Randal Rooney!

HONOR
Oh, thanks! warm from the heart. But here's my father—and where's breakfast?

PHIL
Oh! I must be at him for a horse: you, Honor, mind and back me.

[Enter **OLD McBRIDE**.

OLD McBRIDE
Late I am this fair day all along with my beard, that was thicker than a hedgehog's. Breakfast, where?

HONOR
Here, father dear—all ready.

OLD McBRIDE
There's a jewel! always supple o' foot. Phil, call to them to bring out the horse bastes, while I swallow my breakfast—and a good one, too.

PHIL
Your horse is all ready standing, sir. But that's what I wanted to ax you, father—will you be kind enough, sir, to shell out for me the price of a daacent horse, fit to mount a man like me?

OLD McBRIDE
What ails the baste you have under you always?

PHIL
Fit only for the hounds:—not to follow, but to feed 'em.

OLD McBRIDE
Hounds! I don't want you, Phil, to be following the hounds at-all-at-all.

HONOR
But let alone the hounds. If you sell your bullocks well in the fair to-day, father dear, I think you'll be so kind to spare Phil the price of a horse.

OLD McBRIDE
Stand out o' my way, Honor, with that wheedling voice o' your own—I won't. Mind your own affairs—you're leaguing again me, and I'll engage Randal Rooney's at the bottom of all—and the cement that sticks you and Phil so close together. But mind, Madam Honor, if you give him the meeting at the fair the day—

HONOR
Dear father, I'm not going—I give up the fair o' purpose, for fear I'd see him.

OLD McBRIDE [Kissing her]
Why then you're a piece of an angel!

HONOR
And you'll give my brother the horse?

OLD McBRIDE
I won't! when I've said I won't—I wont.

[Buttons his coat, and exit.

PHIL
Now there's a sample of a father for ye!

OLD McBRIDE [Returning]
And, Mistress Honor, may be you'd be staying at home to—Where's Randal Rooney to be, pray, while I'd be from home?

HONOR
Oh! father, would you suspect—

OLD McBRIDE [Catching her in his arms, and kissing her again and again]
Then you're a true angel, every inch of you. But not a word more in favour of the horse—sure the money for the bullocks shall go to your portion, every farthing.

HONOR
There's the thing!
[Holding her **FATHER**]
I don't wish that.

PHIL [Stopping her mouth]
Say no more, Honor—I'm best pleased so.

OLD McBRIDE [Aside]
I'll give him the horse, but he sha'n't know it.
[Aloud]
I won't. When I say I won't, did I ever?

[Exit **OLD McBRIDE**.

PHIL
Never since the world stud—to do you justice, you are as obstinate as a mule. Not all the bullocks he's carrying to the fair the day, nor all the bullocks in Ballynavogue joined to 'em, in one team, would draw that father o' mine one inch out of his way.

HONOR [Aside, with a deep sigh]
Oh, then what will I do about Randal ever!

PHIL

As close a fisted father as ever had the grip of a guinea! If the guineas was all for you—wilcome, Honor! But that's not it. Pity of a lad o' spirit like me to be cramped by such a hunx of a father.

HONOR

Oh! don't be calling him names, Phil: stiff he is, more than close—and any way, Phil dear, he's the father still—and ould, consider.

PHIL

He is,—and I'm fond enough of him, too, would he only give me the price of a horse. But no matter—spite of him I'll have my swing the day, and it's I that will tear away with a good horse under me and a good whip over him in a capital style, up and down the street of Ballynavogue, for you, Miss Car'line Flaherty! I know who I'll go to, this minute—a man I'll engage will lend me the loan of his bay gelding; and that's Counshillor Gerald O'Blaney.

[Going, **HONOR** stops him.

HONOR

Gerald O'Blaney! Oh, brother!—Mercy!—Don't! any thing rather than that—

PHIL [Impatiently]

Why, then, Honor?

HONOR [Aside]

If I'd tell him, there'd be mischief.
[Aloud]
Only—I wouldn't wish you under a compliment to one I've no opinion of.

PHIL

Phoo! you've taken a prejudice. What is there again Counshillor O'Blaney?

HONOR

Counshillor! First place, why do you call him counshillor? he never was a raal counshillor sure—nor jantleman at all.

PHIL

Oh! counshillor by courtesy—he was an attorney once—just as we doctor the apotecary.

HONOR

But, Phil, was not there something of this man's being dismissed the courts for too sharp practice?

PHIL

But that was long ago, if it ever was. There's sacrets in all families to be forgotten—bad to be raking the past. I never knew you so sharp on a neighbour, Honor, before:—what ails ye?

HONOR [Sighing]

I can't tell ye.

[Still holding him.

PHIL
Let me go, then!—Nonsense!—the boys of Ballynavogue will be wondering, and Miss Car'line most.

[Exit, singing,

"Oh the boys of Ball'navogue."

[**HONOR**, alone.

HONOR
Oh, Phil! I could not tell it you; but did you but know how that Gerald O'Blaney insulted your shister with his vile proposhals, you'd no more ask the loan of his horse!—and I in dread, whenever I'd be left in the house alone, that that bad man would boult in upon me—and Randal to find him! and Randal's like gunpowder when his heart's touched!—and if Randal should come by himself, worse again! Honor, where would be your resolution to forbid him your presence? Then there's but one way to be right—I'll lave home entirely. Down, proud stomach! You must go to service, Honor McBride. There's Mrs. Carver, kind-hearted lady, is wanting a girl—she's English, and nice; may be I'd not be good enough; but I can but try, and do my best; any thing to plase the father.

[Exit **HONOR**.

SCENE II

O'Blaney's Counting-house.

GERALD O'BLANEY alone at a desk covered with Papers.

O'BLANEY
Of all the employments in life, this eternal balancing of accounts, see-saw, is the most sickening of all things, except it would be the taking the inventory of your stock, when you're reduced to invent the stock itself;—then that's the most lowering to a man of all things! But there's one comfort in this distillery business—come what will, a man has always proof spirits.

[Enter **PAT COXE**.

PAT
The whole tribe of Connaught men come, craving to be ped for the oats, counsellor, due since last Serapht (1) fair.

(Footnote 1: Shrovetide)

O'BLANEY

Can't be ped to-day, let 'em crave never so.—Tell 'em Monday; and give 'em a glass of whiskey round, and that will send 'em off contint, in a jerry.

PAT
I shall—I will—I see, sir.

[Exit **PAT COXE**.

O'BLANEY
Asy settled that!—but I hope many more duns for oats won't be calling on me this day, for cash is not to be had:—here's bills plenty—long bills, and short bills—but even the kites, which I can fly as well as any man, won't raise the wind for me now.

[Re-enter **PAT**.

PAT
Tim McGudikren, sir, for his debt—and talks of the sub-sheriff, and can't wait.

O'BLANEY
I don't ax him to wait; but he must take in payment, since he's in such a hurry, this bill at thirty-one days, tell him.

PAT
I shall tell him so, plase your honour.

[Exit **PAT**.

O'BLANEY
They have all rendezvous'd to drive me mad this day; but the only thing is to keep the head cool. What I'm dreading beyant all is, if that ould Matthew McBride, who is as restless as a ferret when he has lodged money with any one, should come this day to take out of my hands the two hundred pounds I've got of his—Oh, then I might shut up! But stay, I'll match him—and I'll match myself too: that daughter Honor of his is a mighty pretty girl to look at, and since I can't get her any other way, why not ax her in marriage? Her portion is to be—

[Re-enter **PAT**.

PAT
The protested note, sir—with the charge of the protest to the back of it, from Mrs. Lorigan; and her compliments, and to know what will she do?

O'BLANEY
What will I do, fitter to ax. My kind compliments to Mrs. Lorigan, and I'll call upon her in the course of the day, to settle it all.

PAT
I understand, sir.

[Exit **PAT**.

O'BLANEY
Honor McBride's portion will be five hundred pounds on the nail—that would be no bad hit, and she a good, clever, likely girl. I'll pop the question this day.

[Re-enter **PAT**.

PAT
Corkeran the cooper's bill, as long as my arm.

O'BLANEY
Oh! don't be bothering me any more. Have you no sinse? Can't you get shut of Corkeran the cooper without me? Can't ye quarrel with the items? Tear the bill down the middle, if necessary, and sind him away with a flay *(flea)* in his ear, to make out a proper bill—which I can't see till to-morrow, mind. I never pay any man on fair-day.

PAT [Aside]
Nor on any other day.
[Aloud]
Corkeran's my cousin, counsellor, and if convanient, I'd be glad you'd advance him a pound or two on account.

O'BLANEY
'Tis not convanient was he twenty times your cousin, Pat. I can't be paying in bits, nor on account—all or none.

PAT
None, then, I may tell him, sir?

O'BLANEY
You may—you must; and don't come up for any of 'em any more. It's hard if I can't have a minute to talk to myself.

PAT
And it's hard if I can't have a minute to eat my breakfast, too, which I have not.

[Exit **PAT**.

O'BLANEY
Where was I?—I was popping the question to Honor McBride. The only thing is, whether the girl herself wouldn't have an objection:—there's that Randal Rooney is a great bachelor of hers, and I doubt she'd be apt to prefar him before me, even when I'd purpose marriage. But the families of the Rooneys and McBrides is at vareance—then I must keep 'em so. I'll keep Catty Rooney's spirit up, niver to consent to that match. Oh! if them Rooneys and McBrides were by any chance to make it up, I'd be undone: but against that catastrophe I've a preventative. Pat Coxe! Pat Coxe! where are you, my young man?

[Enter **PAT**, wiping his mouth.

PAT
Just swallowing my breakfast.

O'BLANEY
Mighty long swallowing you are. Here—don't be two minutes, till you're at Catty Rooney's, and let me see how cliverly you'll execute that confidential embassy I trusted you with. Touch Catty up about her ould ancient family, and all the Kings of Ireland she comes from. Blarney her cliverly, and work her to a foam against the McBrides.

PAT
Never fear, your honour. I'll tell her the story we agreed on, of Honor McBride meeting of Randal Rooney behind the chapel.

O'BLANEY
That will do—don't forget the ring; for I mane to put another on the girl's finger, if she's agreeable, and knows her own interest. But that last's a private article. Not a word of that to Catty, you understand.

PAT
Oh! I understand—and I'll engage I'll compass Catty, tho' she's a cunning shaver.

O'BLANEY
Cunning?—No; she's only hot tempered, and asy managed.

PAT
Whatever she is, I'll do my best to plase you. And I expict your honour, counsellor, won't forget the promise you made me, to ask Mr. Carver for that little place—that situation that would just shute me.

O'BLANEY
Never fear, never fear. Time enough to think of shuting you, when you've done my business.

[Exit **PAT**.

That will work like harm, and ould Matthew, the father, I'll speak to, myself, genteelly. He will be proud, I warrant, to match his daughter with a gentleman like me. But what if he should smell a rat, and want to be looking into my affairs? Oh! I must get it sartified properly to him before all things, that I'm as safe as the bank; and I know who shall do that for me—my worthy friend, that most consequential magistrate, Mr. Carver of Bob's Fort, who loves to be advising and managing of all men, women, and children, for their good. 'Tis he shall advise ould Matthew for my good. Now Carver thinks he lades the whole county, and ten mile round—but who is it lades him, I want to know? Why, Gerald O'Blaney.— And how? Why, by a spoonful of the universal panacea, flattery—in the vulgar tongue, flummery.
[A knock at the door heard]
Who's rapping at the street?—Carver of Bob's Fort himself, in all his glory this fair-day. See then how he struts and swells. Did ever man, but a pacock, look so fond of himself with less rason? But I must be caught deep in accounts, and a balance of thousands to credit.
[Sits down to his desk, to account books]
Seven thousand, three hundred, and two pence.
[Starting and rising]

Do I see Mr. Carver of Bob's Fort?—Oh! the honour—

MR CARVER
Don't stir, pray—I beg—I request—I insist. I am by no means ceremonious, sir.

O'BLANEY [Bustling and setting two chairs]
No, but I'd wish to show respect proper to him I consider the first man in the county.

MR CARVER [Aside]
Man! gentleman, he might have said.

[**MR CARVER** sits down and rests himself consequentially.

O'BLANEY
Now, Mr. Carver of Bob's Fort, you've been over fartiguing yourself—

MR CARVER
For the public good. I can't help it, really.

O'BLANEY
Oh! but, upon my word and honour, it's too much: there's rason in all things. A man of Mr. Carver's fortin to be slaving! If you were a man in business, like me, it would be another thing. I must slave at the desk to keep all round. See, Mr. Carver, see!—ever since the day you advised me to be as particular as yourself in keeping accounts to a farthing, I do, to a fraction, even like state accounts, see!

MR CARVER
And I trust you find your advantage in it, sir. Pray, how does the distillery business go on?

O'BLANEY
Swimmingly! ever since that time, Mr. Carver, your interest at the castle helped me at the dead lift, and got that fine took off. 'Tis to your purtiction, encouragement, and advice entirely, I owe my present unexampled prosperity, which you prophesied; and Mr. Carver's prophecies seldom, I may say never, fail to be accomplished.

MR CARVER
I own there is some truth in your observation. I confess I have seldom been mistaken or deceived in my judgment of man, woman, or child.

O'BLANEY
Who can say so much?

MR CARVER
For what reason, I don't pretend to say; but the fact ostensibly is, that the few persons I direct with my advice are unquestionably apt to prosper in this world.

O'BLANEY
Mighty apt! for which rason I would wish to trouble you for your unprecedently good advice on another pint, if it, would not be too great a liberty.

MR CARVER

No liberty at all, my good Gerald—I am always ready to advise—only to-day—certainly, the fair day of Ballynavogue, there are so many calls upon me, both in a public and private capacity, so much business of vital importance!

O'BLANEY [Aside]

Vital importance!—that is his word on all occasions.
[Aloud]
May be then, (oh! where was my head?) may be you would not have breakfasted all this time? and we've the kittle down always in this house,
[Rising]
Pat!—Jack!—Mick!—Jenny! put the kittle down.

MR CARVER

Sit down, sit still, my worthy fellow. Breakfasted at Bob's Fort, as I always do.

O'BLANEY

But a bit of cake—a glass of wine, to refresh and replinish nature.

MR CARVER

Too early—spoil my dinner. But what was I going to say?

O'BLANEY [Aside]

Burn me, if I know; and I pray all the saints you may never recollect.

MR CARVER

I recollect. How many times do you think I was stopped on horseback coming up the street of Ballynavogue?—Five times by weights and measures imperiously calling for reformation, sir. Thirteen times, upon my veracity, by booths, apple-stalls, nuisances, vagabonds, and drunken women. Pigs without end, sir—wanting ringing, and all squealing in my ears, while I was settling sixteen disputes about tolls and customs. Add to this, my regular battle every fair-day with the crane, which ought to be any where but where it is; and my perputual discoveries of fraudulent kegs, and stones in the butter! Now, sir, I only ask, can you wonder that I wipe my forehead?

[He wipes his forehead.

O'BLANEY

In troth, Mr. Carver, I cannot! But these are the pains and penalties of being such a man of consequence as you evidently are;—and I that am now going to add to your troubles too by consulting you about my little pint!

MR CARVER

A point of law, I dare to say; for people somehow or other have got such a prodigious opinion of my law.

[Takes snuff.

O'BLANEY [Aside]

No coming to the pint till he has finished his own panygeric.

MR CARVER
And I own I cannot absolutely turn my back on people. Yet as to poor people, I always settle them by telling them, it is my principle that law is too expensive for the poor: I tell them, the poor have nothing to do with the laws.

O'BLANEY
Except the penal.

MR CARVER
True, the civil is for us, men of property; and no man should think of going to law, without he's qualified. There should be licenses.

O'BLANEY
No doubt. Pinalties there are in plinty; still those who can afford should indulge. In Ireland it would as ill become a gentleman to be any way shy of a law-shute, as of a duel.

MR CARVER
Yet law is expensive, sir, even to me.

O'BLANEY
But 'tis the best economy in the end; for when once you have cast or non-shuted your man in the courts, 'tis as good as winged him in the field. And suppose you don't get sixpence costs, and lose your cool hundred by it, still it's a great advantage; for you are let alone to enjoy your own in pace and quiet ever after, which you could not do in this county without it. But the love of the law has carried me away from my business: the pint I wanted to consult you about is not a pint of law; 'tis another matter.

MR CARVER [Looking at his watch]
I must be at Bob's Fort, to seal my despatches for the castle. And there's another thing I say of myself.

O'BLANEY [Aside]
Remorseless agotist!

MR CARVER
I don't know how the people all have got such an idea of my connexions at the castle, and my influence with his Excellency, that I am worried with eternal applications: they expect I can make them all gaugers or attorney-generals, I believe. How do they know I write to the castle?

O'BLANEY
Oh! the post-office tells asy by the big sales *(seals)* to your despatches—
[Aside]
—which, I'll engage, is all the castle ever, rades of them, though Carver has his Excellency always in his mouth, God help him!

MR CARVER
Well, you wanted to consult me, Gerald?

O'BLANEY

And you'll give me your advice, which will be conclusive, law, and every thing to me. You know the McBrides—would they be safe?

MR CARVER

Very safe, substantial people.

O'BLANEY

Then here's the thing, Mr. Carver: as you recommend them, and as they are friends of yours—I will confess to you that, though it might not in pint of interest be a very prudent match, I am thinking that Honor McBride is such a prudent girl, and Mrs. Carver has taken her by the hand, so I'd wish to follow Mrs. Carver's example for life, in taking Honor by the hand for better for worse.

MR CARVER

In my humble opinion you cannot do better; and I can tell you a secret—Honor will have no contemptible fortune in that rank of life.

O'BLANEY

Oh, fortune's always contemptible in marriage.

MR CARVER

Fortune! sir?

O'BLANEY [Aside]

Overshot.

[Aloud]

In comparison with the patronage and protection or countenance she'd have from you and your family, sir.

MR CARVER

That you may depend upon, my good Gerald, as far as we can go; but you know we are nothing.

O'BLANEY

Oh, I know you're every thing—every thing on earth—particularly with ould McBride; and you know how to speak so well and iloquent, and I'm so tongue-tied and bashful on such an occasion.

MR CARVER

Well, well, I'll speak for you.

O'BLANEY

A thousand thanks down to the ground.

MR CARVER [Patting him on the back as he rises]

My poor Gerald.

O'BLANEY

Then I am poor Gerald in point of wit, I know; but you are too good a friend to be calling me poor to ould McBride—you can say what I can't say.

MR CARVER

Certainly, certainly; and you may depend on me. I shall speak my decided opinion; and I fancy McBride has sense enough to be ruled by me.

O'BLANEY

I am sure he has—only there's a Randal Rooney, a wild young man, in the case. I'd be sorry the girl was thrown I away upon Randal.

MR CARVER

She has too much sense: the father will settle that, and I'll settle the father.

[**MR CARVER** going.

O'BLANEY [Following, aside]
And who has settled you?

MR CARVER

Don't stir—don't stir—men of business must be nailed to a spot—and I'm not ceremonious.

[Exit **MR CARVER**.

O'BLANEY
Pinned him by all that's cliver!

[Exit **O'BLANE**Y.

SCENE III

Mrs Carver's Dressing-room.

MRS CARVER sitting at work.—**BLOOMSBURY** standing.

BLOOMSBURY

Certainly, ma'am, what I always said was, that for the commonalty, there's no getting out of an Irish cabin a girl fit to be about a lady such as you, Mrs. Carver, in the shape of a waiting-maid or waiting-maid's assistant, on account they smell so of smoke, which is very distressing; but this Honor McBride seems a bettermost sort of girl, ma'am; if you can make up your mind to her vice.

MRS CARVER
Vice?

BLOOMSBURY
That is, vicious pronounciations in regard to their Irish brogues.

MRS CARVER

Is that all?—I am quite accustomed to the accent.

BLOOMSBURY
Then, ma'am, I declare now, I've been forced to stuff my hears with cotton wool hever since I comed to Ireland. But this here Honor McBride has a mighty pretty vice, if you don't take exceptions to a little nationality; nor she if not so smoke-dried: she's really a nice, tidy-looking like girl considering. I've taken tea with the family often, and they live quite snug for Hirish. I'll assure you, ma'am, quite bettermost people for Hibernians, as you always said, ma'am.

MRS CARVER
I have a regard for old Matthew, though he is something of a miser, I fear.

BLOOMSBURY
So, ma'am, shall I call the girl up, that we may see and talk to her? I think, ma'am, you'll find she will do; and I reckon to keep her under my own eye and advice from morning till night: for when I seed the girl so willing to larn, I quite took a fancy to her, I own—as it were.

MRS CARVER
Well, Bloomsbury, let me see this Honor McBride.

BLOOMSBURY [Calling]
One of you there! please call up Honor McBride.

MRS CARVER
She has been waiting a great while, I fear; I don't like to keep people waiting.

BLOOMSBURY [Watching for **HONOR** as she speaks]
Dear heart, ma'am, in this here country, people does love waiting for waiting's sake, that's sure—they got nothing else to do. Here, Honor—walk in, Honor,—rub your shoes always.

[Enter **HONOR**, timidly.

MRS CARVER [In an encouraging voice]
Come in, my good girl.

BLOOMSBURY
Oh! child, the door: the peoples never shut a door in, Ireland! Did not I warn you?—says I, "Come when you're called—do as you're bid—shut the door after you, and you'll never be chid." Now what did I tell you, child?

HONOR
To shut the door after me when I'd come into a room.

BLOOMSBURY
When I'd come—now that's not dic'snary English.

MRS CARVER
Good Bloomsbury, let that pass for the present—come a little nearer to me, my good girl.

HONOR
Yes, ma'am.

BLOOMSBURY
Take care of that china pyramint with your cloak—walk on to Mrs. Carver—no need to be afraid—I'll stand your friend.

MRS CARVER
I should have thought, Honor McBride, you were in too comfortable a way at home, to think of going into service.

HONOR [Sighs]
No better father, nor brother, nor than I have, ma'am, I thank your ladyship; but some things come across.

MRS CARVER [Aside]
Oh! it is a blushing case, I see: I must talk to her alone, by-and-by.
[Aloud]
I don't mean, my good girl, to pry into your family affairs.

HONOR
Oh! ma'am, you're too good.
[Aside]
The kind-hearted Lady, how I love her already!

[She wipes the tears from her eyes.

BLOOMSBURY
Take care of the bow-pot at your elbow, child; for if you break the necks of them moss roses—

HONOR
I ax their pardon.

MRS CARVER
Better take the flower-pot out of her way, Bloomsbury.

BLOOMSBURY [Moving the flower-pot]
There, now: but, Honor, keep your eyes on my lady, never turn your head, and keep your hands always afore you, as I show you. Ma'am, she'll larn manners in time—Lon'on was not built in a day. It i'n't to be expected of she!

MRS CARVER
It is not to be expected indeed that she should learn every thing at once; so one thing at a time, good Bloomsbury, and one person at a time. Leave Honor to me for the present.

BLOOMSBURY
Certainly, ma'am; I beg pardon—I was only saying—

MRS CARVER
Since it is, it seems, necessary, my good girl, that you should leave home, I am glad that you are not too proud to go into service.

HONOR
Oh! into your service, ma'am,—I'd be too proud if you'd be kind enough to accept me.

MRS CARVER
Then as to wages, what do you expect?

HONOR
Any thing at all you please, ma'am.

BLOOMSBURY [Pressing down her shoulder]
And where's your curtsy? We shall bring these Irish knees into training by and by, I hopes.

HONOR
I'm awk'ard and strange, ma'am—I never was from home afore.

MRS CARVER
Poor girl—we shall agree very well, I hope.

HONOR
Oh yes, any thing at all, ma'am; I'm not greedy—nor needy, thanks above! but it's what I'd wish to be under your protection if it was plasing, and I'll do my very best, madam.

[Curtsies.

MRS CARVER
Nobody can expect more, and I hope and trust you'll find mine an easy place—Bloomsbury, you will tell her, what will be required of her.
[**MRS CARVER** looks at her watch]
At twelve o'clock I shall be returned from my walk, and then, Honor, you will come into my cabinet here; I want to say a few words to you.

[Exeunt **OMNES**.

SCENE IV

The High Road—A Cottage in view—Turf-stack, Hay-rick, &c.

CATTY ROONEY alone, walking backwards and forwards.

CATTY

'Tis but a stone's throw to Ballynavogue. But I don't like to be going into the fair on foot, when I been always used to go in upon my pillion behind my husband when living, and my son Randal, after his death. Wait, who comes here?—'Tis Gerald O'Blaney's, the distiller's, young man, Pat Coxe: now we'll larn all—and whether O'Blaney can lend me the loan of a horse or no. A good morrow to you, kindly, Mr. Pat Coxe.

[Enter **PAT COXE**.

PAT
And you the same, Mrs. Rooney, tinfold. Mr. O'Blaney has his sarvices to you, ma'am: no, not his sarvices, but his compliments, that was the word—his kind compliments, that was the very word.

CATTY
The counshillor's always very kind to me, and genteel.

PAT
And was up till past two in the morning, last night, madam, he bid me say, looking over them papers you left with him for your shuit, ma'am, with the McBrides, about the bit of Ballynascraw bog; and if you call upon the counshillor in the course of the morning, he'll find, or make, a minute, for a consultation, he says. But mane time, to take no step to compromise, or make it up, for your life, ma'am.

CATTY
No fear, I'll not give up at law, or any way, to a McBride, while I've a drop of blood in my veins—and it's good thick Irish blood runs in these veins.

PAT
No doubt, ma'am—from the kings of Ireland, as all the world knows, Mrs. Rooney.

CATTY
And the McBrides have no blood at-all-at-all.

PAT
Not a drop, ma'am—so they can't stand before you.

CATTY
They ought not, any way!—What are they? Cromwellians at the best. Mac Brides! Scotch!—not Irish native, at-all-at-all. People of yesterday, graziers—which tho' they've made the money, can't buy the blood. My anshestors sat on a throne, when the McBrides had only their hunkers (1) to sit upon; and if I walk now when they ride, they can't look down upon me—for every body knows who I am—and what they are.

(Footnote 1: Their hunkers, i.e. their hams)

PAT
To be sure, ma'am, they do—the whole country talks of nothing else, but the shame when you'd be walking and they riding.

CATTY

Then could the counshillor lend me the horse?

PAT
With all the pleasure in life, ma'am, only every horse he has in the world is out o' messages, and drawing turf and one thing or another to-day—and he is very sorry, ma'am.

CATTY
So am I, then—I'm unlucky the day. But I won't be saying so, for fear of spreading ill luck on my faction. Pray now what kind of a fair is it?—Would there be any good signs of a fight, Mr. Pat Coxe?

PAT
None in life as yet, ma'am—only just buying and selling. The horse-bastes, and horned-cattle, and pigs squeaking, has it all to themselves. But it's early times yet—it won't be long so.

CATTY
No McBrides, no Ballynavogue boys gathering yet?

PAT
None to signify of the McBrides, ma'am, at all.

CATTY
Then it's plain them McBrides dare not be showing their faces, or even their backs, in Ballynavogue. But sure all our Ballynascraw boys, the Roonies, are in it as usual, I hope?

PAT
Oh, ma'am, there is plinty of Roonies. I marked Big Briny of Cloon, and Ulick of Eliogarty, and little Charley of Killaspugbrone.

CATTY
All good men (1)—no better. Praise be where due.

(Footnote 1: men who fight well)

PAT
And scarce a McBride I noticed. But the father and son—ould Matthew, and flourishing Phil, was in it, with a new pair of boots and the silver-hilted whip.

CATTY
The spalpeen! turned into a buckeen, that would be a squireen,—but can't.

PAT
No, for the father pinches him.

CATTY
That's well—and that ould Matthew is as obstinate a neger as ever famished his stomach. What's he doing in Ballynavogue the day?

PAT

Standing he is there, in the fair-green with his score of fat bullocks, that he has got to sell.

CATTY
Fat bullocks! Them, I reckon, will go towards Honor McBride's portion, and a great fortin she'll be for a poor man—but I covet none of it for me or mine.

PAT
I'm sure of that, ma'am,—you would not demane yourself to the likes.

CATTY
Mark me, Pat Coxe, now—with all them fat bullocks at her back, and with all them fresh roses in her cheeks—and I don't say but she's a likely girl, if she wa'n't a McBride; but with all that, and if she was the best spinner in the three counties—and I don't say but she's good, if she wa'n't a McBride;—but was she the best of the best, and the fairest of the fairest, and had she to boot the two stockings full of gould, Honor McBride shall never be brought home, a daughter-in-law to me! My pride's up.

PAT [Aside]
And I'm instructed to keep it up.—
[Aloud]
True for ye, ma'am, and I wish that all had as much proper pride, as ought to be having it.

CATTY
There's maning in your eye, Pat—give it tongue.

PAT
If you did not hear it, I suppose there's no truth in it.

CATTY
What?—which?

PAT
That your son Randal, Mrs. Rooney, is not of your way of thinking about Honor McBride, may be's.

CATTY
Tut! No matter what way of thinking he is—a young slip of a boy like him does not know what he'll think to-morrow. He's a good son to me; and in regard to a wife, one girl will do him as well as another, if he has any sinse—and I'll find him a girl that will plase him, I'll engage.

PAT
May be so, ma'am—no fear: only boys do like to be plasing themselves, by times—and I noticed something.

CATTY
What did you notice?—till me, Pat, dear, quick.

PAT
No—'tis bad to be meddling and remarking to get myself ill-will; so I'll keep myself to myself: for Randal's ready enough with his hand as you with the tongue—no offence, Mrs. Rooney, ma'am.

CATTY

Niver fear—only till me the truth, Pat, dear.

PAT

Why, then, to the best of my opinion, I seen Honor McBride just now giving Randal Rooney the meeting behind the chapel; and I seen him putting a ring on her finger.

CATTY [Clasping her hands]

Oh, murder!—Oh! the unnat'ral monsters that love makes of these young men; and the traitor, to use me so, when he promised he'd never make a stolen match unknown'st to me.

PAT

Oh, ma'am, I don't say—I wouldn't swear—it's a match yet.

CATTY

Then I'll run down and stop it—and catch 'em.

PAT

You haven't your jock on, ma'am—
[She turns towards the house]
—and it's no use—for you won't catch 'em: I seen them after, turning the back way into Nick Flaherty's.

CATTY

Nick Flaherty's, the publican's? oh, the sinners! And this is the saint that Honor McBride would be passing herself upon us for? And all the edication she got at Mrs. Carver's Sunday school! Oh, this comes of being better than one's neighbours! A fine thing to tell Mrs. Carver, the English lady, that's so nice, and so partial to Miss Honor McBride! Oh, I'll expose her!

PAT

Oh! sure, Mrs. Rooney, you promised you'd not tell,

[Standing so as to stop **CATTY**.

CATTY

Is it who told me? No—I won't mintion a sintence of your name. But let me by—I won't be put off now I've got the scent. I'll hunt 'em out, and drag her to shame, if they're above ground, or my name's not Catty Rooney! Mick! Mick! little Mick!
[Calling at the cottage door]
—bring my blue jock up the road after me to Ballynavogue. Don't let me count three till you're after me, or I'll bleed ye!

[Exit **CATTY**, shaking her closed hand, and repeating]
I'll expose Honor McBride—I'll expose Honor! I will, by the blessing!

PAT [Alone]

Now, if Randal Rooney would hear, he'd make a jelly of me, and how I'd trimble; or the brother, if he comed across me, and knewed. But they'll niver know. Oh, Catty won't say a sintence of my name, was she carded! No, Catty's a scould, but has a conscience. Then I like conscience in them I have to dale with sartainly.

[Exit.

SCENE V

Mrs Carver's Dressing-room, **HONOR McBRIDE** and **MISS BLOOMSBURY** discovered.

HONOR
How will I know, Miss Bloomsbury, when it will be twelve o'clock?

BLOOMSBURY
You'll hear the clock strike: but I suspect you'se don't understand the clock yet—well, you'll hear the workmen's bell.

HONOR
I know, ma'am, oh, I know, true—only I was flurried, so I forgot.

BLOOMSBURY
Flurried! but never be flurried. Now mind and keep your head upon your shoulders, while I tell you all your duty—you'll just ready this here room, your lady's dressing-room; not a partical of dust let me never find, petticlarly behind the vindor shuts.

HONOR
Vindor shuts!—where, ma'am?

BLOOMSBURY
The shuts of the vindors—did you never hear of a vindor, child?

HONOR
Never, ma'am.

BLOOMSBURY [Pointing to a window]
Don't tell me! why, your head is a wool-gathering! Now, mind me, pray—see here, always you put that there,—and this here, and that upon that,—and this upon this, and this under that,—and that under this—you can remember that much, child, I supposes?

HONOR
I'll do my endeavour, ma'am, to remember all.

BLOOMSBURY
But mind, now, my good girl, you takes petticlar care of this here pyramint of japanned china—and very petticlar care of that there great joss—and the very most petticularest care of this here right reverend Mandolin.

[Pointing to, and touching a Mandarin, so as to make it shake. **HONOR** starts back.

BLOOMSBURY
It i'n't alive. Silly child, to start at a Mandolin shaking his head and beard at you. But, oh! mercy, if there i'n't enough to make him shake his head. Stand there!—stand here!—now don't you see?

HONOR
Which, ma'am?

BLOOMSBURY
"Which, ma'am!" you're no witch, indeed, if you don't see a cobweb as long as my arm. Run, run, child, for the pope's head.

HONOR
Pope's head, ma'am?

BLOOMSBURY
Ay, the pope's head, which you'll find under the stairs. Well, a'n't you gone? what do you stand there like a stuck pig, for?—Never see a pope's head?—never 'ear of a pope's head?

HONOR
I've heard of one, ma'am—with the priest; but we are protestants.

BLOOMSBURY
Protestants! what's that to do? I do protest, I believe that little head of yours is someway got wrong on your shoulders to-day.

[The clock strikes—**HONOR**, who is close to it, starts.

BLOOMSBURY
Start again!—why, you're all starts and fits. Never start, child! so ignoramus like! 'tis only the clock in your ear,—twelve o'clock, hark!—The bell will ring now in a hurry. Then you goes in there to my lady— stay, you'll never be able, I dare for to say, for to open the door without me; for I opine you are not much usen'd to brass locks in Hirish cabins—can't be expected. See here, then! You turns the lock in your hand this'n ways—the lock, mind now; not the key nor the bolt for your life, child, else you'd bolt your lady in, and there'd be my lady in Lob's pound, and there'd be a pretty kettle, of fish!—So you keep, if you can, all I said to you in your head, if possible—and you goes in there—and I goes out here.

[Exit **BLOOMSBURY**.

HONOR [Curtsying]
Thank ye, ma'am. Then all this time I'm sensible I've been behaving and looking little better than like a fool, or an innocent.—But I hope I won't be so bad when the lady shall speak to me.

[The bell rings.

Oh, the bell summons me in here.—
[Speaks with her hand on the lock of the door]

The lock's asy enough—I hope I'll take courage—
[Sighs]
—Asier to spake before one nor two, any way—and asier tin times to the mistress than the maid.

[Exit **HONOR.**

Gerald O'Blaney's Counting-house.

O'BLANEY alone.

O'BLANEY
Then I wonder that ould Matthew McBride is not here yet. But is not this Pat Coxe coming up yonder? Ay. Well, Pat, what success with Catty?

[Enter **PAT COXE**, panting.

Take breath, man alive—What of Catty?

PAT
Catty! Oh, murder! No time to be talking of Catty now! Sure the shupervizor's come to town.

O'BLANEY
Blood!—and the malt that has not paid duty in the cellar! Run, for your life, to the back-yard, give a whistle to call all the boys that's ricking o' the turf, away with 'em to the cellar, out with every sack of malt that's in it, through the back-yard, throw all into the middle of the turf-stack, and in the wink of an eye build up the rick over all, snoog *(snug).*

PAT
I'll engage we'll have it done in a crack.

[Exit **PAT.**

O'BLANEY [Calling after him]
Pat! Pat Coxe! man!

[Re-enter **PAT.**

O'BLANEY
Would there be any fear of any o' the boys informin?

PAT
Sooner cut their ears off!

[Exit **PAT**.

[Enter **OLD McBRIDE**, at the opposite side.

OLD McBRIDE [Speaking in a slow, drawling brogue]
Would Mr. Gerald O'Blaney, the counsellor, be within?

O'BLANEY [Quick brogue]
Oh, my best friend, Matthew McBride, is it you, dear? Then here's Gerald O'Blaney, always at your sarvice. But shake hands; for of all men in Ireland, you are the man I was aching to lay my eyes on. And in the fair did ye happen to meet Carver of Bob's Fort?

OLD McBRIDE [Speaking very slowly]
Ay. did I—and he was a-talking to me, and I was a-talking to him—and he's a very good gentleman, Mr. Carver of Bob's Fort—so he is—and a gentleman that knows how things should be; and he has been giving of me, Mr. O'Blaney, a great account of you, and how you're thriving in the world—and so as that.

O'BLANEY
Nobody should know that better than Mr. Carver of Bob's Fort—he knows all my affairs. He is an undeniable honest gentleman, for whom I profess the highest regard.

OLD McBRIDE
Why then he has a great opinion of you too, counsellor—for he has been advising of, and telling of me, O'Blaney, of your proposhal, sir—and very sinsible I am of the honour done by you to our family, sir—and condescension to the likes of us—though, to be sure, Honor McBride, though she is my daughter, is a match for any man.

O'BLANEY
Is a match for a prince—a Prince Ragent even. So no more about condescension, my good Matthew, for love livels all distinctions.

OLD McBRIDE
That's very pretty of you to say so, sir; and I'll repeat it to Honor.

O'BLANEY
Cupid is the great liveller, after all, and the only democrat Daity on earth I'd bow to—for I know you are no democrat, Mr. McBride, but quite and clane the contrary way.

OLD McBRIDE
Quite and clane and stiff, I thank my God; and I'm glad, in spite of the vowel before your name, Mr. O'Blaney, to hear you are of the same kidney.

O'BLANEY
I'm happy to find myself agreeable to you, sir.

OLD McBRIDE

But, however agreeable to me, as I won't deny, it might be, sir, to see my girl made into a gentlewoman by marriage, I must observe to you—

O'BLANEY
And I'll keep her a jaunting car to ride about the country; and in another year, as my fortune's rising, my wife should rise with it into a coach of her own.

OLD McBRIDE
Oh! if I'd live to see my child, my Honor, in a coach of her own! I'd be too happy—oh, I'd die contint!

O'BLANEY [Aside]
No fear!—
[Aloud]
And why should not she ride in her own coach, Mistress Counsellor O'Blaney, and look out of the windows down upon the Roonies, that have the insolence to look up to her?

OLD McBRIDE
Ah! you know that, then. That's all that's against us, sir, in this match.

O'BLANEY
But if you are against Randal, no fear.

OLD McBRIDE
I am against him—that is, against his family, and all his seed, breed, and generation. But I would not break my daughter's heart if I could help it.

O'BLANEY
Wheugh!—hearts don't break in these days, like china.

OLD McBRIDE
This is my answer, Mr. O'Blaney, sir: you have my lave, but you must have hers too.

O'BLANEY
I would not fear to gain that in due time, if you would stand my friend in forbidding her the sight of Randal.

OLD McBRIDE
I will with pleasure, that—for tho' I won't force her to marry to plase me, I'll forbid her to marry to displase me; and when I've said it, whatever it is, I'll be obeyed.

[Strikes his stick on the ground.

O'BLANEY
That is all I ax.

OLD McBRIDE
But now what settlement, counshillor, will you make on my girl?

O'BLANEY

A hundred a year—I wish to be liberal—Mr. Carver will see to that—he knows all my affairs, as I suppose he was telling you.

OLD McBRIDE

He was—I'm satisfied, and I'm at a word myself always. You heard me name my girl's portion, sir?

O'BLANEY

I can't say—I didn't mind—'twas no object to me in life.

OLD McBRIDE [In a very low, mysterious tone, and slow brogue]
Then five hundred guineas is some object to most men.

O'BLANEY

Certainly, sir; but not such an object as your daughter to me: since we are got upon business, however, best settle all that out of the way, as you say at once. Of the five hundred, I have two in my hands already, which you can make over to me with a stroke of a pen.

[Rising quickly, and getting pen, ink, and books.

OLD McBRIDE [Speaking very slowly]
Stay a hit—no hurry—in life. In business—'tis always most haste, worse speed.

O'BLANEY

Take your own time, my good Matthew—I'll be as slow as you plase—only love's quick.

OLD McBRIDE

Slow and sure—love and all—fast bind, fast find—three and two, what does that make?

O'BLANEY

It used to make five before I was in love.

OLD McBRIDE

And will the same after you're married and dead. What am I thinking of? A score of bullocks I had in the fair—half a score sold in my pocket, and owing half—that's John Dolan, twelve pound tin—and Charley Duffy nine guineas and thirteen tin pinnies and a five-penny bit: stay, then, put that to the hundred guineas in the stocking at home.

O'BLANEY [Aside]
How he makes my mouth water:
[Aloud]
May be, Matthew, I could, that am used to it, save you the trouble of counting?

OLD McBRIDE

No trouble in life to me ever to count my money—only I'll trouble you, sir, if you please, to lock that door; bad to be chinking and spreading money with doors open, for walls has ears and eyes.

O'BLANEY

True for you.

[Rising, and going to lock the doors.

[**OLD McBRIDE** with great difficulty, and very slowly, draws out of his pocket his bag of money—looking first at one door, and then at the other, and going to try whether they are locked, before he unties his bag.}

OLD McBRIDE [Spreads and counts his money and notes]
See me now, I wrote on some scrap somewhere 59l. in notes—then hard cash, twenty pounds—rolled up silver and gould, which is scarce—but of a hundred pounds there's wanting fourteen pounds odd, I think, or something that way; for Phil and I had our breakfast out of a one pound note of Finlay's, and I put the change somewhere—besides a riband for Honor, which make a deficiency of fourteen pounds seven shillings and two pence—that's what's deficient—count it which way you will.

O'BLANEY [Going to sweep the money off the table]
Oh! never mind the deficiency—I'll take it for a hundred plump.

OLD McBRIDE [Stopping him]
Plump me no plumps—I'll have it exact, or not at all—I'll not part it, so let me see it again.

O'BLANEY [Aside with a deep sigh, almost a groan]
Oh! when I had had it in my fist—almost: but 'tis as hard to get money out of this man as blood out of a turnip; and I'll be lost to-night without it.

OLD McBRIDE
'Tis not exact—and I'm exact: I'll put it all up again—
[He puts it deliberately into the bag again, thrusting the bag into his pocket]
—I'll make it up at home my own way, and send it in to you by Phil in an hour's time; for I could not sleep sound with so much in my house—bad people about—safer with you in town. Mr. Carver says, you are as good as the Bank of Ireland—there's no going beyond that.
[Buttoning up his pockets]
So you may unlock the doors and let me out now—I'll send Phil with all to you, and you'll give him a bit of a receipt or a token, that would do.

O'BLANEY
I shall give a receipt by all means—all regular: short accounts make long friends.

[Unlocks the door.

OLD McBRIDE
True, sir, and I'll come in and see about the settlements in the morning, if Honor is agreeable.

O'BLANEY
I shall make it my business to wait upon the young lady myself on the wings of love; and I trust I'll not find any remains of Randal Rooney in her head.

OLD McBRIDE

Not if I can help it, depend on that.

[They shake hands.

O'BLANEY
Then, fare ye well, father-in-law—that's meat and drink to me: would not ye take a glass of wine then?

OLD McBRIDE
Not a drop—not a drop at all—with money about me: I must be in a hurry home.

O'BLANEY
That's true—so best: recommind me kindly to Miss Honor, and say a great dale about my impatience—and I'll be expicting Phil, and won't shut up till he comes the night.

OLD McBRIDE
No, don't; for he'll be with you before night-fall.

[Exit **OLD McBRIDE**.

O'BLANEY [Calling]
Dan! open the door, there: Dan! Joe! open the door smart for Mr. McBride!

[**O'BLANEY** rubbing his hands.

Now I think I may pronounce myself made for life—success to my parts!—and here's Pat too! Well, Pat Coxe, what news of the thing in hand?

[Enter **PAT COXE**.

PAT
Out of hand clane! that job's nately done. The turf-rick, sir, 's built up cliver, with the malt snug in the middle of its stomach—so were the shupervishor a conjuror even, barring he'd dale with the ould one, he'd never suspect a sentence of it.

O'BLANEY
Not he—he's no conjuror: many's the dozen tricks I played him afore now.

PAT
But, counshillor, there's the big veshel in the little passage—I got a hint from a friend, that the shuper got information of the spirits in that from some villain.

O'BLANEY
And do you think I don't know a trick for that, too?

PAT
No doubt: still, counshillor, I'm in dread of my life that that great big veshel won't be implied in a hurry.

O'BLANEY

Won't it? but you'll see it will, though; and what's more, them spirits will turn into water for the shupervisor.

PAT
Water! how?

O'BLANEY
Asy—the ould tan-pit that's at the back of the distillery.

PAT
I know—what of it?

O'BLANEY
A sacret pipe I've got fixed to the big veshel, and the pipe goes under the wall for me into the tan-pit, and a sucker I have in the big veshel, which I pull open by a string in a crack, and lets all off all clane into the tan-pit.

PAT
That's capital!—but the water?

O'BLANEY
From the pump, another pipe—and the girl's pumping asy, for she's to wash to-morrow, and knows nothing about it; and so the big veshel she fills with water, wondering what ails the water that it don't come—and I set one boy and another to help her—and the pump's bewitched, and that's all:—so that's settled.

PAT
And cliverly. Oh! counshillor, we are a match for the shuper any day or night.

O'BLANEY
For him and all his tribe, coursing officers and all. I'd desire no better sport than to hear the whole pack in full cry after me, and I doubling, and doubling, and safe at my form at last. With you, Pat, my precious, to drag the herring over the ground previous to the hunt, to distract the scent, and defy the nose of the dogs.

PAT
Then I am proud to sarve you, counshillor.

O'BLANEY
I know you are, and a very honest boy. And what did you do for me, with Catty Rooney?

PAT
The best.—Oh! it's I blarny'd Catty to the skies, and then egged her on, and aggravated her against the McBrides, till I left her as mad as e'er a one in Bedlam—up to any thing! And full tilt she's off to Flaherty's, the publican, in her blue jock—where she'll not be long afore she kicks up a quarrel, I'll engage; for she's sarching the house for Honor McBride, who is not in it—and giving bad language, I warrant, to all the McBride faction, who is in it, drinking. Oh! trust Catty's tongue for breeding a riot! In half an hour, I'll warrant, you'll have as fine a fight in town as ever ye seen or hard.

O'BLANEY
That's iligantly done, Pat. But I hope Randal Rooney is in it?

PAT
In the thick of it he is, or will be. So I hope your honour did not forgit to spake to Mr. Carver about that little place for me?

O'BLANEY
Forgit!—Do I forgit my own name, do you think? Sooner forgit that then my promises.

PAT
Oh! I beg your honour's pardon—I would not doubt your word; and to make matters sure, and to make Catty cockahoop, I tould her, and swore to her, there was not a McBride in the town but two, and there's twinty, more or less.

O'BLANEY
And when she sees them twinty, more or less, what will she think?—Why would you say that?—she might find you out in a lie next minute, Mr. Overdo. 'Tis dangerous for a young man to be telling more lies than is absolutely requisite. The lie superfluous brings many an honest man, and, what's more, many a cliver fellow, into a scrape—and that's your great fau't, Pat.

PAT
Which, sir?

O'BLANEY
That, sir. I don't see you often now take a glass too much. But, Pat, I hear you often still are too apt to indulge in a lie too much.

PAT
Lie! Is it I?—Whin upon my conscience, I niver to my knowledge tould a lie in my life, since I was born, excipt it would be just to skreen a man, which is charity, sure,—or to skreen myself, which is self-defence, sure—and that's lawful; or to oblige your honour, by particular desire, and that can't be helped, I suppose.

O'BLANEY
I am not saying again all that—only—
[Laying his hand on **PAT'S** shoulder as he is going out]
—against another time, all I'm warning you, young man, is, you're too apt to think there never can be lying enough. Now too much of a good thing is good for nothing.

[Exit **O'BLANEY**.

[**PAT**, alone.

PAT
There's what you may call the divil rebuking sin—and now we talk of the like, as I've heard my mudther say, that he had need of a long spoon that ates wid the divil—so I'll look to that in time. But whose voice

is that I hear coming up stairs? I don't believe but it's Mr. Carver—only what should bring him back agin, I wonder now? Here he is, all out of breath, coming.

[Enter **MR CARVER**.

MR CARVER
Pray, young man, did you happen to see—
[Panting for breath]
Bless me, I've ridden so fast back from Bob's Fort!

PAT
My master, sir, Mr. O'Blaney, is it? Will I run?

MR CARVER
No, no—stand still till I have breath.—What I want is a copy of a letter I dropped some where or other—here I think it must have been, when I took out my handkerchief—a copy of a letter to his Excellency—of great consequence.

[**MR CARVER** sits down and takes breath.

PAT [Searching about with officious haste]
If it's above ground, I'll find it. What's this?—an old bill: that is not it. Would it be this, crumpled up?—"To His Excellency the Lord Lieutenant of Ireland."

MR CARVER [Snatching]
No farther, for your life!

PAT
Well then I was lucky I found it, and proud.

MR CARVER
And well you may be, young man; for I can assure you, on this letter the fate of Ireland may depend.

[Smoothing the letter on his knee.

PAT
I wouldn't doubt it—when it's a letter of your honour's—I know your honour's a great man at the castle. And plase your honour, I take this opportunity of tanking your honour for the encouragement I got about that little clerk's place—and here's a copy of my hand-writing I'd wish to show your honour, to see I'm capable—and a scholard.

MR CARVER
Hand-writing! Bless me, young man, I have no time to look at your hand-writing, sir. With the affairs of the nation on my shoulders—can you possibly think?—is the boy mad?—that I've time to revise every poor scholar's copy-book?

PAT

I humbly beg your honour's pardon, but it was only becaase I'd wish to show I was not quite so unworthy to be under (whin you've time) your honour's protection, as promised.

MR CARVER

My protection?—you are not under my protection, sir:—promised clerk's place?—I do not conceive what you are aiming at, sir.

PAT

The little clerk's place, plase your honour—that my master, Counshillor O'Blaney, tould me he spoke about to your honour, and was recommending me for to your honour.

MR CARVER

Never—never heard one syllable about it, till this moment.

PAT

Oh! murder:—but I expict your honour's goodness will—

MR CARVER

To make your mind easy, I promised to appoint a young man to that place, a week ago, by Counsellor O'Blaney's special recommendation. So there must be some mistake.

[Exit **MR CARVER**.

[**PAT**, alone.

PAT

Mistake? ay, mistake on purpose. So he never spoke! so he lied!—my master that was praching me! And oh, the dirty lie he tould me! Now I can't put up with that, when I was almost perjuring myself for him at the time. Oh, if I don't fit him for this! And he got the place given to another!—then I'll git him as well sarved, and out of this place too—seen-if-I-don't! He is cunning enough, but I'm cuter nor he—I have him in my power, so I have! and I'll give the shupervizor a scent of the malt in the turf-stack—and a hint of the spirits in the tan-pit—and it's I that will like to stand by innocent, and see how shrunk O'Blaney's double face will look forenent the shupervizor, when all's found out, and not a word left to say, but to pay—ruined hand and foot! Then that shall be, and before nightfall. Oh! one good turn desarves another—in revenge, prompt payment while you live!

[Exit.

SCENE II

McBride's Cottage.

MATTHEW McBRIDE and **HONOR**.

MATTHEW with a little table before him, at dinner.

OLD McBRIDE [Pushing his plate from him]
I'll take no more—I'm done.

[He sighs.

HONOR
Then you made but a poor dinner, father, after being at the fair, and up early, and all!—Take this bit from my hands, father dear.

OLD McBRIDE [Turning away sullenly]
I'll take nothing from you, Honor, but what I got already enough—and too much of—and that's ungratitude.

HONOR
Ungratitude, father! then you don't see my heart.

OLD McBRIDE
I lave that to whoever has it, Honor: 'tis enough for me, I see what you do—and that's what I go by.

HONOR
Oh, me! and what did I do to displase you, father?
[He is obstinately silent; after waiting in vain for an answer, she continues]
I that was thinking to make all happy,—
[Aside]
—but myself,—
[Aloud]
—by settling to keep out of the way of—all that could vex you—and to go to sarvice, to Mrs. Carver's. I thought that would plase you, father.

OLD McBRIDE
Is it to lave me, Honor? Is it that you thought would plase me, Honor?—To lave your father alone in his ould age, after all the slaving he got and was willing to undergo, whilst ever he had strength, early and late, to make a little portion for you, Honor,—you, that I reckoned upon for the prop and pride of my ould age—and you expect you'd plase me by laving me.

HONOR
Hear me just if, pray then, father.

OLD McBRIDE [Shaking her off as she tries to caress him]
Go, then; go where you will, and demane yourself going into sarvice, rather than stay with me—go.

HONOR
No, I'll not go. I'll stay then with you, father dear,—say that will plase you.

OLD McBRIDE [Going on without listening to her]
And all for the love of this Randal Rooney! Ay, you may well put your two hands before your face; if you'd any touch of natural affection at all, that young man would have been the last of all others you'd ever have thought of loving or liking any way.

HONOR
Oh! if I could help it!

OLD McBRIDE
There it is. This is the way the poor fathers is always to be trated. They to give all, daughter and all, and get nothing at all, not their choice even of the man, the villain that's to rob 'em of all—without thanks even; and of all the plinty of bachelors there are in the parish for the girl that has money, that daughter will go and pick and choose out the very man the father mislikes beyond all others, and then it's "Oh! if I could help it!"—Asy talking!

HONOR
But, dear father, wasn't it more than talk, what I did?—Oh, won't you listen to me?

OLD McBRIDE
I'll not hear ye; for if you'd a grain o spirit in your mane composition, Honor, you would take your father's part, and not be putting yourself under Catty's feet—the bad-tongued woman, that hates you, Honor, like poison.

HONOR
If she does hate me, it's all through love of her own—

OLD McBRIDE
Son—ay—that she thinks too good for you—for you, Honor; you, the Lily of Lismore—that might command the pride of the country. Oh! Honor dear, don't be lessening yourself; but be a proud girl, as you ought, and my own Honor.

HONOR
Oh, when you speak so kind!

OLD McBRIDE
And I beg your pardon, if I said a cross word; for I know you'll never think of him more, and no need to lave home at all for his sake. It would be a shame in the country, and what would Mrs. Carver herself think?

HONOR
She thinks well of it, then.

OLD McBRIDE
Then whatever she thinks, she sha'n't have my child from me! tho' she's a very good lady, and a very kind lady, too. But see now, Honor—have done with love, for it's all foolishness; and when you come to be as ould as I am, you'll think so too. The shadows goes all one way, till the middle of the day, and when that is past, then all the t'other way; and so it is with love, in life—stay till the sun is going down with you.

HONOR
Then it would be too late to be thinking of love.

OLD McBRIDE

And too airly now, and there's no good time, for it's all folly. I'll ax you, will love set the potatoes?—will love make the rent?—or will love give you a jaunting car?—as to my knowledge, another of your bachelors would.

HONOR

Oh, don't name him, father.

OLD McBRIDE

Why not—when it's his name that would make a lady of you, and there'd be a rise in life, and an honour to your family?

HONOR

Recollect it was he that would have dishonoured my family, in me, if he could.

OLD McBRIDE

But he repints now; and what can a man do but repint, and offer to make honourable restitution, and thinking of marrying, as now, Honor dear;—is not that a condescension of he, who's a sort of a jantleman?

HONOR

A sort, indeed—a bad sort.

OLD McBRIDE

Why, not jantleman born, to be sure.

HONOR

Nor bred.

OLD McBRIDE

Well, there's many that way, neither born nor bred, but that does very well in the world; and think what it would be to live in the big shingled house, in Ballynavogue, with him!

HONOR

I'd rather live here with you, father.

OLD McBRIDE

Then I thank you kindly, daughter, for that, but so would not I for you,—and then the jaunting-car, or a coach, in time, if he could! He has made the proposhal for you in form this day.

HONOR

And what answer from you, father?

OLD McBRIDE

Don't be looking so pale,—I tould him he had my consint, if he could get yours. And, oh! before you speak, Honor dear, think what it would be up and down in Ballynavogue, and every other place in the county, assizes days and all, to be Mistress Gerald O'Blaney!

HONOR
I couldn't but think very ill of it, father; thinking ill, as I do, of him. Father dear, say no more, don't be breaking my heart—I'll never have that man; but I'll stay happy with you.

OLD McBRIDE
Why, then, I'll be contint with that same; and who wouldn't?—If it's what you'd rather stay, and can stay contint, Honor dear, I'm only too happy.
[Embracing her—then pausing]
But for Randal—

HONOR
In what can you fau't him, only his being a Rooney?

OLD McBRIDE
That's all—but that's enough. I'd sooner see you in your coffin—sooner be at your wake to-night, than your wedding with a Rooney! 'Twould kill me. Come, promise me—I'd trust your word—and 'twould make me asy for life, and I'd die asy, if you'd promise never to have him.

HONOR
Never till you would consent—that's all I can promise.

OLD McBRIDE
Well, that same is a great ase to my heart.

HONOR
And to give a little ase to mine, father, perhaps you could promise—

OLD McBRIDE
What?—I'll promise nothing at all—I'll promise nothing at all—I'll promise nothing I couldn't perform.

HONOR
But this you could perform asy, dear father: just hear your own Honor.

OLD McBRIDE [Aside]
That voice would wheedle the bird off the bush—and when she'd prefar me to the jaunting-car, can I but listen to her?
[Aloud]
Well, what?—if it's any thing at all in rason.

HONOR
It is in rason entirely. It's only, that if Catty Rooney's—

OLD McBRIDE [Stopping his ears]
Don't name her.

HONOR
But she might be brought to rason, father; and if she should be brought to give up that claim to the bit o' bog of yours, and when all differs betwix' the families be made up, then you would consent.

OLD McBRIDE
When Catty Rooney's brought to rason! Oh! go shoe the goslings, dear,—ay, you'll get my consint then. There's my hand: I promise you, I'll never be called on to perform that, Honor, jewel.

HONOR [Kissing his hand]
Then that's all I'd ask—nor will I say one word more, but thank you, father.

OLD McBRIDE [Putting on his coat]
She's a good cratur—sorrow better! sister or daughter. Oh! I won't forget that she prefarred me to the jaunting-car. Phil shall carry him a civil refusal. I'll send off the money, the three hundred, by your brother, this minute—that will be some comfort to poor O'Blaney.

[Exit **McBRIDE**.

HONOR
Is not he a kind father, then, after all?—That promise he gave me about Catty, even such as it is, has ased my heart wonderfully. Oh! it will all come right, and they'll all be rasonable in time, even Catty Rooney, I've great hope; and little hope's enough, even for love to live upon. But, hark! there's my brother Phil coming.
[A noise heard in the back-house]
'Tis only the cow in the bier.
[A knock heard at the door]
No, 'tis a Christian; no cow ever knocked so soft. Stay till I open—Who's in it?

RANDAL [From within]
Your own Randal—open quick.

HONOR
Oh! Randal, is it you? I can't open the door.

[She holds the door—he pushes it half open.

RANDAL
Honor, that I love more than life, let me in, till I speak one word to you, before you're set against me for ever.

HONOR
No danger of that—but I can't let you in, Randal.

RANDAL
Great danger! Honor, and you must. See you I will, if I die for it!

[He advances, and she retires behind the door, holding it against him.

HONOR
Then I won't see you this month again, if you do. My hand's weak, but my heart's strong, Randal.

RANDAL
Then my heart's as weak as a child's this minute. Never fear—don't hold against me, Honor; I'll stand where I am, since you don't trust me, nor love me—and best so, may be: I only wanted to say three words to you.

HONOR
I can't hear you now, Randal.

RANDAL
Then you'll never hear me more. Good bye to you, Honor.

[He pulls the door to, angrily.

HONOR
And it's a wonder as it was you didn't meet my father as you came, or my brother.

RANDAL [Pushing the door a little open again]
Your brother!—Oh, Honor! that's what's breaking my heart—
[He sighs]
—that's what I wanted to say to you; and listen to me. No fear of your father, he's gone down the road: I saw him as I come the short cut, but he didn't see me.

HONOR
What of my brother?—say, and go.

RANDAL
Ay, go—for ever, you'll bid me, when I've said.

HONOR
What! oh, speak, or I'll drop.—

[She no longer holds the door, but leans against a table.—**RANDAL** advances, and looks in.

RANDAL
Don't be frightened, then, dearest—it's nothing in life but a fight at a fair. He's but little hurted.

HONOR
Hurted!—and by who? by you, is it?—Then all's over.—

[**RANDAL** comes quite in—**HONOR**, putting her hand before her eyes.

—You may come or go, for I'll never love you more.

RANDAL
I expicted as much!—But she'll faint!

HONOR
I won't faint: leave me, Mr. Randal.

RANDAL
Take this water from me,—
[Holding a cup]
—it's all I ask.

HONOR
No need.
[She sits down]
But what's this?—

[Seeing his hand bound up.

RANDAL
A cut only.

HONOR
Bleeding—stop it.

[Turning from him coldly.

RANDAL
Then by this blood—no, not by this worthless blood of mine—but by that dearest blood that fled from your cheeks, and this minute is coming back, Honor, I swear—

[Kneeling to her.

HONOR
Say what you will, or swear, I don't hear or heed you. And my father will come and find you there—and I don't care.

RANDAL
I know you don't—and I don't care myself what happens me. But as to Phil, it's only a cut in the head he got, that signifies nothing—if he was not your brother.

HONOR
Once lifted your hand against him—all's over.

RANDAL
Honor, I did not lift my hand against him; but I was in the quarrel with his faction.

HONOR
And this your promise to me not to be in any quarrel! No, if my father consented to-morrow, I'd nivir have you now.

[Rises, and is going—he holds her.)

RANDAL

Then you're wrong, Honor: you've heard all against me—now hear what's for me.

HONOR
I'll hear no more—let me go.

RANDAL
Go, then;—
[He lets her go, and turns away himself]
—and I'm going before Mr. Carver, who will hear me, and the truth will appear—and tho' not from you, Honor, I'll have justice.

[Exit **RANDAL**.

HONOR
Justice! Oh, worse and worse! to make all public; and if once we go to law, there's an end of love—for ever.

[Exit **HONOR**.

SCENE III

O'Blaney's House.

O'BLANEY and **CATTY ROONEY**.

CATTY
And didn't ye hear it, counshillor? the uproar in the town and the riot?—oh! you'd think the world was throwing out at windows. See my jock, all tattered! Didn't ye hear!

O'BLANEY
How could I hear, backwards, as you see, from the street, and given up to my business?

CATTY
Business! oh! here is a fine business—the McBrides have driven all before them, and chased the Roonies out of Ballynavogue.
[In a tone of deep despair]
Oh! Catty Rooney! that ever you'd live to see this day!

O'BLANEY
Then take this glass—
[Offering a glass of whiskey]
—to comfort your heart, my good Mrs. Rooney.

CATTY
No, thank you, counshillor, it's past that even! ogh! ogh!—oh! wirrastrew!—oh! wirrastrew, ogh!—
[After wringing her hands, and yielding to a burst of sorrow and wailing, she stands up firmly]

Now I've ased my heart, I'll do. I've spirit enough left in me yet, you'll see; and I'll tell you what I came to you for, counshillor.

O'BLANEY
Tell me first, is Randal Rooney in it, and is he hurt?

CATTY
He was in it: he's not hurt, more shame for him! But, howsomever, he bet one boy handsomely; that's my only comfort. Our faction's all going full drive to swear examinations, and get justice.

O'BLANEY
Very proper—very proper: swear examinations—that's the course, and only satisfaction in these cases to get justice.

CATTY
Justice!—revenge sure! Oh! revenge is sweet, and I'll have it. Counshillor dear, I never went before Mr. Carver—you know him, sir—what sort is he?

O'BLANEY
A mighty good sort of gentleman—only mighty tiresome.

CATTY
Ay, that's what I hard—that he is mighty fond of talking to people for their good. Now that's what I dread, for I can't stand being talked to for my good.

O'BLANEY
'Tis little use, I confess. We Irish is wonderful soon tired of goodness, if there's no spice of fun along with it; and poor Carver's soft, and between you and I, he's a little bothered, but, Mrs. Rooney, you won't repate?

CATTY
Repate!—I! I'm neither watch nor repater—I scorn both; and between you and I, since you say so, counshillor, that's my chiefest objection to Carver, whom I wouldn't know from Adam, except by reputation. But it's the report of the country, that he has common informers in his pay and favour; now that's mane, and I don't like it.

O'BLANEY
Nor I, Mrs. Rooney. I had experience of informers in the distillery line once. The worst varmin that is ever encouraged in any house or country. The very mintion of them makes me creep all over still.

CATTY
Then 'tis Carver, they say, that has the oil of Rhodium for them; for they follow and fawn on him, like rats on the rat catcher—of all sorts and sizes, he has 'em. They say, he sets them over and after one another; and has lations of them that he lets out on the craturs' cabins, to larn how many grains of salt every man takes with his little prates, and bring information if a straw would be stirring.

O'BLANEY

Ay, and if it would, then, it's Carver that would quake like the aspin leaf—I know that. It's no malice at all in him; only just he's a mighty great poltroon.

CATTY
Is that all? Then I'd pity and laugh at him, and I go to him preferably to any other magistrate.

O'BLANEY
You may, Mrs. Rooney—for it's in terror of his life he lives, continually draming day and night, and croaking of carders and thrashers, and oak boys, and white boys, and peep-o'-day boys, and united boys, and riband-men, and men and boys of all sorts that have, and that have not, been up and down the country since the rebellion.

CATTY
The poor cratur! But in case he'd prove refractory, and would not take my examinations, can't I persecute my shute again the McBrides for the bit of the bog of Ballynascraw, counshillor?—Can't I harash 'em at law?

O'BLANEY
You can, ma'am, harash them properly. I've looked over your papers, and I'm happy to tell you, you may go on at law as soon and as long as you plase.

CATTY [Speaking very rapidly]
Bless you for that word, counshillor; and by the first light to-morrow, I'll drive all the grazing cattle, every four-footed baast off the land, and pound 'em in Ballynavogue; and if they replevy, why I'll distrain again, if it be forty times, I will go. I'll go on distraining, and I'll advertise, and I'll cant, and I'll sell the distress at the end of the eight days. And if they dare for to go for to put a plough in that bit of reclaimed bog, I'll come down upon 'em with an injunction, and I would not value the expinse of bringing down a record a pin's pint; and if that went again me, I'd remove it to the courts above and wilcome; and after that, I'd go into equity, and if the chancillor would not be my friend, I'd take it over to the House of Lords in London, so I would as soon as look at 'em; for I'd wear my feet to the knees for justice—so I would.

O'BLANEY
That you would! You're an iligant lawyer, Mrs. Rooney; but have you the sinews of war?

CATTY
Is it money, dear?—I have, and while ever I've one shilling to throw down to ould Matthew McBride's guinea, I'll go on; and every guinea he parts will twinge his vitals: so I'll keep on while ever I've a fiv'-penny bit to rub on another—for my spirit is up.

O'BLANEY
Ay, ay, so you say. Catty, my dear, your back's asy up, but it's asy down again.

CATTY
Not when I've been trod on as now, counshillor: it's then I'd turn and fly at a body, gentle or simple, like mad.

O'BLANEY

Well done, Catty.
[Patting her on the back]
There's my own pet mad cat—and there's a legal venom in her claws, that every scratch they'll give shall fester so no plaister in law can heal it.

CATTY
Oh, counshillor, now, if you wouldn't be flattering a wake woman.

O'BLANEY
Wake woman!—not a bit of woman's wakeness in ye. Oh, my cat-o'-cats! let any man throw her from him, which way he will, she's on her legs and at him again, tooth and claw.

CATTY
With nine lives, renewable for ever.

[Exit **CATTY**.

O'BLANEY [Alone]
There's a demon in woman's form set to work for me! Oh, this works well—and no fear that the Roonies and McBrides should ever come to an understanding to cut me out. Young Mr. Randal Rooney, my humble compliments to you, and I hope you'll become the willow which you'll soon have to wear for Miss Honor McBride's pretty sake. But I wonder the brother a'n't come up yet with the rist of her fortune.
[Calls behind the scenes]
Mick! Jack! Jenny! Where's Pat?—Then why don't you know? run down a piece of the road towards Ballynascraw, see would you see any body coming, and bring me word would you see Phil McBride—you know, flourishing Phil.—Now I'm prepared every way for the shupervishor, only I wish to have something genteel in my fist for him, and a show of cash flying about—nothing like it, to dazzle the eyes.

[Exit **O'BLANEY**.

ACT III

SCENE I

An Apartment in Mr. Carver's House.

MR CARVER seated: a table, pens, ink, paper, and law-books. A cleric, pen in hand.—On the right-hand side of **MR CARVER** stands **MRS CATTY ROONEY**.—**RANDAL ROONEY** beside her, leaning against a pillar, his arms folded.—Behind **MRS ROONEY**, three men—one remarkably tall, one remarkably little.—On the left-hand of **MR CARVER** stand **OLD MATTHEW McBRIDE**, leaning on his stick; beside him, **PHILIP McBRIDE**, with his silver-hilted whip in his hand.—A Constable at some distance behind Mr. Carver's chair.—**MR CARVER** looking over and placing his books, and seeming to speak to his clerk.

CATTY [Aside to her son]

See I'll take it asy, and be very shivel and sweet wid him, till I'll see which side he'll lane, and how it will go with us Roonies—

[MR CARVER rising, leans forward with both his hands on the table, as if going to speak, looks round, and clears his throat loudly]

—Will I spake now, plase your honour?

OLD McBRIDE
Dacency, when you see his honour preparing his throat.

[MR CARVER clears his throat again.

CATTY [Curtsying between each sentence]
Then I ixpect his honour will do me justice. I got a great character of his honour. I'd sooner come before your honour than any jantleman in all Ireland. I'm sure your honour will stand my frind.

CLERK
Silence!

MR CARVER
Misguided people of Ballynavogue and Ballynascraw—

[At the instant **MR CARVER** pronounces the word "Ballynavogue," **CATTY** curtsies, and all the **ROONIES**, behind her, bow, and answer—

Here, plase your honour.

[And when **MR CARVER** says "Ballynascraw," all the **McBRIDES** bow, and reply—

Here, plase your honour.

MR CARVER [Speaking with pomposity, but embarrassment, and clearing his throat frequently]
When I consider and look round me, gentlemen, and when I look round me and consider, how long a period of time I have had the honour to bear his majesty's commission of the peace for this county—

CATTY [Curtsying]
Your honour's a good warrant, no doubt.

MR CARVER
Hem!—hem!—also being a residentiary gentleman at Bob's Fort—hem!—hem!—hem!—

[He coughs, and blows his nose.

CATTY [Aside to her son]
Choking the cratur is with the words he can't get out.
[Aloud]
Will I spake now, plase your honour?

CLERK
Silence! silence!

MR CARVER
And when I consider all the ineffectual attempts I have made by eloquence and otherwise, to moralize and civilize you gentlemen, and to eradicate all your heterogeneous or rebellious passions—

CATTY
Not a rebel, good or bad, among us, plase your honour.

CLERK
Silence!

MR CARVER
I say, my good people of Ballynavogue and Ballynascraw, I stand here really in unspeakable concern and astonishment, to notice at this fair-time in my barony, these symptoms of a riot, gentlemen, and features of a tumult.

CATTY
True, your honour, see—scarce a symptom of a fature lift in the face here of little Charley of Killaspugbrone, with the b'ating he got from them McBrides, who bred the riot, entirely under Flourishing Phil, plase your honour.

MR CARVER [Turning to **PHIL McBRIDE**]
Mr. Philip McBride, son of old Matthew, quite a substantial man,—I am really concerned, Philip, to see you, whom I looked upon as a sort of, I had almost said, gentleman—

CATTY
Gentleman! what sort? Is it because of the new topped boots, or by virtue of the silver-topped whip, and the bit of a red rag tied about the throat?—Then a gentleman's asy made, now-a-days.

YOUNG McBRIDE
It seems 'tis not so asy any way, now-a-days, to make a gentlewoman, Mrs. Rooney.

CATTY [Springing forward angrily]
And is it me you mane, young man?

RANDAL
Oh! mother, dear, don't be aggravating.

MR CARVER
Clerk, why don't you maintain silence?

CATTY [Pressing before her **SON**]
Stand back, then, Randal Rooney—don't you hear silence?—don't be brawling before his honour. Go back wid yourself to your pillar, or post, and fould your arms, and stand like a fool that's in love, as you are.—I beg your honour's pardon, but he's my son, and I can't help it.—But about our examinations,

plase your honour, we're all come to swear—here's myself, and little Charley of Killaspugbrone, and big Briny of Cloon, and Ulick of Eliogarty—all ready to swear.

MR CARVER
But have these gentlemen no tongues of their own, madam?

CATTY
No, plase your honour, little Charley has no English tongue; he has none but the native Irish.

MR CARVER
Clerk, make out their examinations, with a translation; and interpret for Killaspugbrone.

CATTY
Plase your honour, I being the lady, expicted I'd get lave to swear first.

MR CARVER
And what would you swear, madam, if you got leave, pray?—be careful, now.

CATTY
I'll tell you how it was out o' the face, plase your honour. The whole Rooney faction—

MR CARVER
Faction!—No such word in my presence, madam.

CATTY
Oh, but I'm ready to swear to it, plase your honour, in or out of the presence:—the whole Rooney faction—every Rooney, big or little, that was in it, was bet, and banished the town and fair of Ballynavogue, for no rason in life, by them McBrides there, them scum o' the earth.

MR CARVER
Gently, gently, my good lady; no such thing in my presence, as scum o' the earth.

CATTY
Well, Scotchmen, if your honour prefars. But before a Scotchman, myself would prefar the poorest spalpeen—barring it be Phil, the buckeen—I ax pardon—
[Curtsying]
—if a buckeen's the more honourable.

MR CARVER
Irrelevant in toto, madam; for buckeens and spalpeens are manners or species of men unknown to or not cognizable by the eye of the law; against them, therefore, you cannot swear: but if you have any thing against Philip McBride—

CATTY
Oh, I have plinty, and will swear, plase your honour, that he put me in bodily fear, and tore my jock, my blue jock, to tatters. Oh, by the vartue of this book—
[Snatching up a book]

—and all the books that ever were shut or opened, I'll swear to the damage of five pounds, be the same more or less.

MR CARVER
My good lady, more or less will never do.

CATTY
Forty shillings, any way, I'll swear to; and that's a felony, your honour, I hope?

MR CARVER
Take time, and consult your conscience conscientiously, my good lady, while I swear these other men—

[She examines the coat, holding it up to view—**MR CARVER** beckons to the **ROONEY** party.

MR CARVER
Beaten men! come forward.

BIG BRINY
Not beaten, plase your honour, only bet.

ULICK OF ELIOGARTY
Only black eyes, plase your honour.

MR CARVER
You, Mr. Charley or Charles Rooney, of Killaspugbrone; you have read these examinations, and are you scrupulously ready to swear?

CATTY
He is, and will, plase your honour; only he's the boy that has got no English tongue.

MR CARVER
I wish you had none, madam, ha! ha! ha!

[The **TWO McBRIDES** laugh—the **ROONIES** look grave.

You, Ulick Rooney, of Eliogarty, are these your examinations?

CATTY
He can't write, nor rade writing from his cradle, plase your honour; but can make his mark equal to another, sir. It has been read to him any way, sir, plase your honour.

MR CARVER
And you, sir, who style yourself big Briny of Cloon—you think yourself a great man, I suppose?

CATTY
It's what many does that has got less rason, plase your honour.

MR CARVER

Understand, my honest friend, that there is a vast difference between looking big and being great.

BIG BRINY
I see—I know, your honour.

MR CARVER
Now, gentlemen, all of you, before I hand you the book to swear these examinations, there is one thing of which I must warn and apprize you—that I am most remarkably clear-sighted; consequently there can be no thumb kissing with me, gentlemen.

Big Briny. We'll not ax it, plase your honour.

CATTY
No Rooney, living or dead, was ever guilty or taxed with the like!
[Aside to her **SON**]
Oh, they'll swear iligant! We'll flog the world, and have it all our own way! Oh, I knew we'd get justice—or I'd know why.

CLERK
Here's the book, sir, to swear complainants.

[**MR CARVER** comes forward.

MR CARVER
Wait—wait; I must hear both sides.

CATTY
Both sides! Oh, plase your honour—only bother you.

MR CARVER
Madam, it is my duty to have ears for all men.—Mr. Philip, now for your defence.

CATTY
He has none in nature, plase your honour.

MR CARVER
Madam, you have had my ear long enough—be silent, at your peril.

CATTY
Ogh—ogh!—silent!

[She groans piteously.

MR CARVER
Sir, your defence, without any preamble or pre-ambulation.

PHIL
I've no defence to make, plase your honour, but that I'm innocent.

MR CARVER [Shaking his head]
The worst defence in law, my good friend, unless you've witnesses.

PHIL
All present that time in the fair was too busy fighting for themselves to witness for me that I was not; except I'd call upon one that would clear me entirely, which is that there young man on the opposite side.

CATTY
Oh, the impudent fellow! Is it my son?

OLD McBRIDE
Is it Randal Rooney? Why, Phil, are you turned innocent?

PHIL
I am not, father, at all. But with your lave, I call on Randal Rooney, for he is an undeniable honourable man—I refer all to his evidence.

RANDAL
Thank you, **PHIL**
I'll witness the truth, on whatever side.

CATTY [Rushes in between them, exclaiming, in a tremendous tone]
If you do, Catty Rooney's curse be upon—

[**RANDAL** stops her mouth, and struggles to hold his **MOTHER** back.

Oh, mother, you couldn't curse!—

[All the **ROONIES** get about her and exclaim:—

Oh, Catty, your son you couldn't curse!

MR CARVER
Silence, and let me be heard. Leave this lady to me; I know how to manage these feminine vixens. Mrs. Catherine Rooney, listen to me—you are a reasonable woman.

CATTY
I am not, nor don't pretend to it, plase your honour.

MR CARVER
But you can hear reason, madam, I presume, from the voice of authority.

CATTY
No, plase your honour—I'm deaf, stone deaf.

MR CARVER

No trifling with me, madam; give me leave to advise you a little for your good.

CATTY
Plase your honour, it's of no use—from a child up I never could stand to be advised for my good. See, I'd get hot and hotter, plase your honour, till I'd bounce! I'd fly! I'd burst! and myself does not know what mischief I mightn't do.

MR CARVER
Constable! take charge of this cursing and cursed woman, who has not respect for man or magistrate. Away with her out of my presence!—I commit her for a contempt.

RANDAL [Eagerly]
Oh! plase your honour, I beg your honour's pardon for her—my mother—entirely. When she is in her rason, she has the greatest respect for the whole bench, and your honour above all. Oh! your honour, be plasing this once! Excuse her, and I'll go bail for her she won't say another word till she'd get the nod from your honour.

MR CARVER
On that condition, and on that condition only, I am willing to pass over the past. Fall back, constable.

CATTY [Aside]
Why then, Gerald O'Blaney mislet me. This Carver is a fauterer of the Scotch. Bad luck to every bone in his body!

[As **CATTY** says this her **SON** draws her back, and tries to pacify her.

MR CARVER
Is she muttering, constable?

RANDAL
Not a word, plase your honour, only just telling herself to be quiet. Oh, mother, dearest, I'll kneel to plase you.

CATTY
Kneel! oh, to an ould woman like me—no standing that! So here, on my hunkers I am, for your sake, Randal, and not a word, good or bad! Can woman do more?

[She sits with her fingers on her lips.

MR CARVER [Pulling out his watch]
Now for your defence, Philip: be short, for mercy's sake!

PHIL
Not to be detaining your honour too long—I was in Ballynavogue this forenoon, and was just—that is, Miss Car'line Flaherty was just—

MR CARVER
Miss Caroline Flaherty! What in nature can she have to do with the business?

PHIL
Only axing me, sir, she was, to play the flageolets, which was the rason I was sitting at Flaherty's.

MR CARVER
Address yourself to the court, young man.

PHIL
Sitting at Flaherty's—in the parlour, with the door open, and all the McBrides which was in it was in the outer room taking a toombler o' punch I trated 'em to—but not drinking—not a man out o' the way—when in comes that gentlewoman.
[Pointing to **MRS ROONEY**.—**RANDAL** groans]
Never fear, Randal, I'll tell it as soft as I can.

OLD McBRIDE
Soft, why? Mighty soft cratur ever since he was born, plase your honour, though he's my son.

MR CARVER [Putting his fingers on his lips]
Friend Matthew, no reflections in a court of justice ever. Go on, Philip.

PHIL
So some one having tould Mrs. Rooney lies, as I'm confident, sir—for she come in quite mad, and abused my sister Honor; accusing her, before all, of being sitting and giving her company to Randal Rooney at Flaherty's, drinking, and something about a ring, and a meeting behind the chapel, which I couldn't understand;—but it fired me, and I stepped—but I recollected I'd promised Honor not to let her provoke me to lift a hand good or bad—so I stepped across very civil, and I said to her, says I, Ma'am, it's all lies—some one has been belying Honor McBride to you, Mrs. Rooney.

[**CATTY** sighs and groans, striking the back of one hand reiteratedly into the palm of the other—rises—beats the devil's tattoo as she stands—then claps her hands again.

MR CARVER
That woman has certainly more ways of making a noise, without speaking, than any woman upon earth. Proceed, Philip.

PHIL
Depind on it, it's all lies, Mrs. Rooney, says I, ma'am. No, but you lie, flourishing Phil, says she. With that every McBride to a man, rises from the table, catching up chairs and stools and toomblers and jugs to revenge Honor and me. Not for your life, boys, don't let-drive ne'er a one of yees, says I—she's a woman, and a widow woman, and only a scould from her birth: so they held their hands; but she giving tongue bitter, 'twas hard for flesh and blood to stand it. Now, for the love of heaven and me, sit down all, and be quite as lambs, and finish your poonch like gentlemen, sir, says I: so saying, I tuk Mrs. Rooney up in my arms tenderly, as I would a bould child—she screeching and screeching like mad:—whereupon her jock caught on the chair, pocket-hole or something, and give one rent from head to fut—and that was the tattering of the jock. So we got her to the door, and there she spying her son by ill-luck in the street, directly stretches out her' arms, and kicking my shins, plase your honour, till I could not hold her, "Murder! Randal Rooney," cries she, "and will you see your own mother murdered?"

RANDAL
Them were the very words, I acknowledge, she used, which put me past my rason, no doubt.

PHIL
Then Randal Rooney, being past his rason, turns to all them Roonies that were in no condition.

MR CARVER
That were, what we in English would call drunk, I presume?

RANDAL
Something very near it, plase your honour.

PHIL
Sitting on the bench outside the door they were, when Randal came up. "Up, Roonies, and at 'em!" cried he; and up, to be sure, they flew, shillelahs and all, like lightning, daling blows on all of us McBrides: but I never lifted a hand; and Randal, I'll do him justice, avoided to lift a hand against me.

RANDAL
And while I live I'll never forget that hour, nor this hour, Phil, and all your generous construction.

CATTY [Aside]
Why then it almost softens me; but I won't be made a fool on.

MR CARVER [Who has been re-considering the examinations]
It appears to me that you, Mr. Philip McBride, did, as the law allows, only lay hands softly upon complainant, Catherine Rooney; and the Rooneys, as it appears, struck, and did strike, the first blow.

RANDAL
I can't deny, plase your honour, we did.

MR CARVER [Tearing the examinations]
Then, gentlemen—you Roonies—beaten men, I cannot possibly take your examinations.

[When the examinations are torn, the **McBRIDES** all bow and thank his honour.

MR CARVER
Beaten men! depart in peace.

[The **ROONIES** sigh and groan, and after turning their hats several times, bow, walk a few steps away, return, and seem loath to depart. **CATTY** springs forward, holding up her hands joined in a supplicating attitude to **MR CARVER**.

RANDAL
If your honour would be plasing to let her spake now, or she'd burst, may be.

MR CARVER
Speak now, woman, and ever after hold your tongue.

CATTY

Then I am rasonable now, plase your honour; for I'll put it to the test—see, I'll withdraw my examinations entirely, and I'll recant—and I'll go farther, I'll own I'm wrong—though I know I'm right—and I'll beg your pardon, McBrides, if—(but I know I'll not have to beg your pardon either)—but I say I will beg your pardon, McBrides, if, mind if, you will accept my test, and it fails me.

MR CARVER

Very fair, Mrs. Rooney.

OLD McBRIDE

What is it she's saying?

PHIL

What test, Mrs. Rooney?

RANDAL

Dear mother, name your test.

CATTY

Let Honor McBride be summoned, and if she can prove she took no ring, and was not behind the chapel with Randal, nor drinking at Flaherty's with him, the time she was, I give up all.

RANDAL

Agreed, with all the pleasure in life, mother. Oh, may I run for her?

OLD McBRIDE

Not a fut, you sir—go, Phil dear.

PHIL

That I will, like a lapwing, father.

MR CARVER

Where to, sir—where so precipitate?

PHIL

Only to fetch my sister.

MR CARVER

Your sister, sir?—then you need not go far: your sister, Honor McBride, is, I have reason to believe, in this house.

CATTY

So. Under whose protection, I wonder?

MR CARVER

Under the protection of Mrs. Carver, madam, into whose service she was desirous to engage herself; and whose advice—

CLERK
Shall I, if you please, sir, call Honor in?

MR CARVER
If you please.

[A silence.—**CATTY** stands biting her thumb.—**OLD McBRIDE** leans his chin upon Us hands on his stick, and never stirs, even his eyes.—**YOUNG McBRIDE** looks out eagerly to the side at which **HONOR** is expected to enter—**RANDAL** looking over his shoulder, exclaims—

There she comes!—Innocence in all her looks.

CATTY
Oh! that we shall see soon. No making a fool of me.

OLD McBRIDE
My daughter's step—I should know it.
[Aside]
How my old heart bates!

[**MR CARVER** takes a chair out of the way.

CATTY
Walk in—walk on, Miss **HONOR**
Oh, to be sure, Miss Honor will have justice.

[Enter **HONOR McBRIDE**, walking very timidly.

And no need to be ashamed, Miss Honor, until you're found out.

MR CARVER
Silence!

OLD McBRIDE
Thank your honour.

[**MR CARVER** whispers to his clerk, and directs him while the following speeches go on.

CATTY
That's a very pretty curtsy, Miss Honor—walk on, pray—all the gentlemen's admiring you—my son Randal beyant all.

RANDAL
Mother, I won't bear—

CATTY
Can't you find a sate for her, any of yees? Here's a stool—give it her, Randal.

[**HONOR** sits down.

And I hope it won't prove the stool of repentance, Miss or Madam. Oh, bounce your forehead, Randal—truth must out; you've put it to the test, sir.

RANDAL
I desire no other for her or myself.

[The **FATHER** and **BROTHER** take each a hand of **HONOR**—support and soothe her.

CATTY
I'd pity you, Honor, myself, only I know you a McBride—and know you're desaving me, and all present.

MR CARVER
Call that other witness I allude to, clerk, into our presence without delay.

CLERK
I shall, sir.

[Exit **CLERK**.

CATTY
We'll see—we'll see all soon—and the truth will come out, and shame the dibbil and the McBrides!

RANDAL [Looking out]
The man I bet, as I'm a sinner!

CATTY
What?—Which?—Where?—True for ye!—I was wondering I did not see the man you bet appear again ye: and this is he, with the head bound up in the garter, coming—miserable cratur he looks—who would he be?

RANDAL
You'll see all soon, mother.

[Enter **PAT COXE**, his head bound up.

MR CARVER
Come on—walk on boldly, friend.

CATTY
Pat Coxe! saints above!

MR CARVER
Take courage, you are under my protection here—no one will dare to touch you.

RANDAL [With infinite contempt]
Touch ye! Not I, ye dirty dog!

MR CARVER
No, sir, you have done enough that way already, it appears.

HONOR
Randal! what, has Randal done this?

MR CARVER
Now observe—this Mr. Patrick Coxe, aforesaid, has taken refuge with me; for he is, it seems, afraid to appear before his master, Mr. O'Blaney, this night, after having been beaten: though, as he assures me, he has been beaten without any provocation whatsoever, by you, Mr. Randal Rooney—answer, sir, to this matter.

RANDAL
I don't deny it, sir—I bet him, 'tis true.

PAT
To a jelly—without marcy—he did, plase your honour, sir.

RANDAL
Sir, plase your honour, I got rason to suspect this man to be the author of all them lies that was tould backwards and forwards to my mother, about me and Miss Honor McBride, which made my mother mad, and driv' her to raise the riot, plase your honour. I charged Pat with the lies, and he shirked, and could give me no satisfaction, but kept swearing he was no liar, and bid me keep my distance, for he'd a pocket pistol about him. "I don't care what you have about you—you have not the truth about ye, nor in ye," says I; "ye are a liar, Pat Coxe," says I: so he cocked the pistol at me, saying, that would prove me a coward—with that I wrenched the pistol from him, and bet him in a big passion. I own to that, plase your honour—there I own I was wrong—
[Turning to **HONOR**]
—to demane myself lifting my hand any way.

MR CARVER
But it is not yet proved that this man has told any lies.

RANDAL
If he has tould no lies, I wronged him. Speak, mother—
[COXE gets behind **CATTY**, and twitches her gown]
—was it he who was the informer, or not?

CATTY
Nay, Pat Coxe, if you lied, I'll not screen you; but if you tould the truth, stand out like a man, and stand to it, and I'll stand by you, against my own son even, Randal, if he was the author of the report. In plain words, then, he, Pat Coxe, tould me, that she, Honor McBride, gave you, Randal Rooney, the meeting behind the chapel, and you gave her the ring—and then she went with you to drink at Flaherty's.

HONOR [Starting up]
Oh! who could say the like of me?

CATTY
There he stands—now, Pat, you must stand or fall—will you swear to what you said?

[**OLD McBRIDE** and **PHIL** approach **PAT**.

MR CARVER
This is not the point before me; but, however, I waive that objection.

RANDAL
Oh! mother, don't put him to his oath, lest he'd perjure himself.

PAT
I'll swear: do you think I'd be making a liar of myself?

HONOR
Father—Phil dear—hear me one word!

RANDAL
Hear her—oh! hear her—go to her.

HONOR [In a low voice]
Would you ask at what time it was he pretends I was taking the ring and all that?

OLD McBRIDE
Plase your honour, would you ask the rascal what time?

MR CARVER
Don't call him rascal, sir—no rascals in my presence. What time did you see Honor McBride behind the chapel, Pat Coxe?

PAT
As the clock struck twelve—I mind—by the same token the workmen's bell rang as usual! that same time, just as I seen Mr. Randal there putting the ring on her finger, and I said, "There's the bell ringing for a wedding," says I.

MR CARVER
To whom did you say that, sir?

PAT
To myself, plase your honour—I'll tell you the truth.

HONOR
Truth! That time the clock struck twelve and the bell rang, I was happily here in this house, sir.

HONOR
If I might take the liberty to call one could do me justice.

MR CARVER

No liberty in justice—speak out.

HONOR
If I might trouble Mrs. Carver herself?

MR CARVER
Mrs. Carver will think it no trouble—
[Rising with dignity]
—to do justice, for she has been the wife to one of his majesty's justices of the peace for many years.

[Sends a **SERVANT** for **MRS CARVER**.

MR CARVER
Mrs. Carver, my dear, I must summon you to appear in open court, at the suit or prayer of Honor McBride.

[Enter **MRS CARVER**, who is followed by **MISS BLOOMSBURY**, on tiptoe.

MRS CARVER
Willingly.

MR CARVER
The case lies in a nutshell, my dear: there is a man who swears that Honor McBride was behind the chapel, with Randal Rooney putting a ring on her finger, when the clock struck twelve, and our workmen's bell rang this morning. Honor avers she was at Bob's Fort with you: now as she could not be, like a bird, in two places at once—was she with you?

MRS CARVER
Honor McBride was with me when the workmen's bell rang, and when the clock struck twelve, this day—she stayed with me till two o'clock.

[All the **ROONIES**, except **CATTY**, exclaim—

Oh, no going beyond the lady's word!

MRS CARVER
And I think it but justice to add, that Honor McBride has this day given me such proofs of her being a good girl, a good daughter, and a good sister, that she has secured my good opinion and good wishes for life.

MR CARVER
And mine in consequence.

BLOOMSBURY
And mine of course.

[**HONOR** curtsies.

[OLD McBRIDE bows very low to **MR CARVER**, and again to **MRS CARVER**. **PHIL** bows to **MR AND MRS CARVER**, and to **MISS BLOOMSBURY**.

OLD McBRIDE
Where are you now, Catty?—and you, Pat, ye unfortinate liar?

PAT [Falling on his knees]
On me knees I am. Oh, I am an unfortinate liar, and I beg your honour's pardon this once.

MR CARVER
A most abandoned liar, I pronounce you.

PAT
Oh! I hope your honour won't abandon me, for I didn't know Miss Honor was under her ladyship, Mrs. Carver's favour and purtection, or I'd sooner ha' cut my tongue out clane—and I expict your honour won't turn your hack on me quite, for this is the first lies I ever was found out in since my creation; and how could I help, when it was by my master's particular desire?

MR CARVER
Your master! honest Gerald O'Blaney!

CATTY [Lifting up her hands and eyes]
O'Blaney!—save us!

MR CARVER
Take care, Pat Coxe.

PAT
Mr. O'Blaney, ma'am—plase your honour—all truth now—the counshillor, that same and no other, as I've breath in my body—for why should I tell a lie now, when I've no place in my eye, and not a ha'porth to get by it? I'll confess all. It was by my master's orders that I should set you, Mrs. Rooney, and your pride up, ma'am, again' making up with them McBrides. I'll tell the truth now, plase your honour—that was the cause of the lies I mentioned about the ring and chapel—I'll tell more, if you'll bind Mr. Randal to keep the pace.

RANDAL
I?—ye dirty dog!—Didn't I tell ye already, I'd not dirty my fingers with the likes of you?

PAT
All Mr. Gerald O'Blaney's aim was to ruin Mr. Randal Rooney, and set him by the ears with that gentleman, Mr. Philip McBride, the brother, and they to come to blows and outrage, and then be in disgrace committed by his honour.

RANDAL [Turning to **HONOR McBRIDE**]
Honor, you saved all—your brother and I never lifted our hands against one another, thanks be to Heaven and you, dearest!

CATTY

And was there no truth in the story of the chapel and the ring?

PAT
Not a word of truth, but lies, Mrs. Rooney, dear ma'am, of the master's putting into my mouth out of his own head.

[CATTY ROONEY walks firmly and deliberately across the room to **HONOR McBRIDE**.

CATTY
Honor McBride, I was wrong; and here, publicly, as I traduced you, I ax your pardon before his honour, and your father, and your brother, and before Randal, and before my faction and his.

[Both **ROONIES** and **McBRIDES** all, excepting **OLD McBRIDE**, clap their hands, and huzza.

MR CARVER
I ought to reprove this acclamation—but this once I let it pass.

PHIL
Father, you said nothing—what do you say, sir?

OLD McBRIDE [Never moving]
I say nothing at all. I never doubted Honor, and knew the truth must appear—that's all I say.

HONOR
Oh! father dear—more you will say—
[Shaking his stick gently]
Look up at me, and remember the promise you gave me, when Catty should be rasonable—and is not she rasonable now?

OLD McBRIDE
I did not hear a word from her about the bog of Ballynascraw.

CATTY
Is it the pitiful bit?—No more about it! Make crame cheeses of it—what care I? 'Twas only for pride I stood out—not that I'm thinking of now!

OLD McBRIDE
Well, then, miracles will never cease! here's one in your favour, Honor; so take her, Randal, fortune and all—a wife of five hundred.

RANDAL [Kneeling]
Oh! happiest of men I am this minute.

CATTY
I the same, if she had not a pinny in the world.

MR CARVER

Happiest of men!—Don't kneel or go in to ecstasies now, I beg, till I know the rationale of this. Was not I consulted?—did not I give my opinion and advice in favour of another?

OLD McBRIDE
You was—you did, plase your honour, and I beg your honour's pardon, and Mr. Counsellor O'Blaney's.

MR CARVER
And did not you give your consent?—I must think him a very ill-used person.

OLD McBRIDE
I gave my consint only in case he could win hers, plase your honour, and he could not—and I could not break my own daughter's heart, and I beg your honour's pardon.

MR CARVER
I don't know how that may be, sir, but I gave my approbation to the match; and I really am not accustomed to have my advice or opinion neglected or controverted. Yet, on the other hand—

[Enter a **FOOTMAN** with a note, which he gives to **MR CARVER**.

OLD McBRIDE [Aside to **PHIL**]
Say something for me, Phil, can't ye?—I hav'n't a word.

MR CARVER [Rising with a quicker motion than usual]
Bless me! bless me!—here is a revolution! and a counter revolution!—Here's news will make you all in as great astonishment as I own I am.

OLD McBRIDE
What is it?

RANDAL
I'm made for life—I don't care what comes.

HONOR
Nor I: so it is not to touch you, I'm happy.

CATTY
Oh! your honour, spake quick, this time—I beg pardon!

MR CARVER
Then I have to confess that for once I have been deceived and mistaken in my judgment of a man; and what is more, of a man's circumstances completely—O'Blaney.

OLD McBRIDE
What of his circumstances, oh! sir, in the name of mercy?

MR CARVER
Bankrupt, at this instant all under seizure to the supervisor. Mr. Gerald O'Blaney has fled the country.

OLD McBRIDE
Then, Honor, you are without a penny; for all her fortune, 500l., was in his hands.

RANDAL
Then I'm as happy to have her without a penny—happier I am to prove my love pure.

CATTY
God bless you for my own son! That's our way of thinking, Mr. McBride—you see it was not for the fortune.

HONOR
Oh! Phil, didn't I tell you her heart was right?

CATTY
We will work hard—cheer up, McBrides. Now the Roonies and McBrides has joined, you'll see we'll defy the world and O'Blaney, the chate of chates.

HONOR
Randal's own mother!

CATTY
Ay, now, we are all one family—now pull together. Don't be cast down, Phil dear. I'll never call you flourishing Phil again, so don't be standing on pride. Suppose your shister has not a pinny, she's better than the best, and I'll love her and fold her to my ould warm heart, and the daughter of my heart she is now.

HONOR
Oh, mother!—for you are my mother now—and happy I am to have a mother in you.

MR CARVER
I protest it makes me almost—almost—blow my nose.

CATTY
Why, then, you're a good cratur. But who tould you I was a vixen, dear—plase your honour?

MR CARVER
Your friend that is gone.

CATTY
O'Blaney?

RANDAL
Frind! He never was frind to none—least of all to hisself.

CATTY
Oh! the double-distilled villain!—he tould your honour I was a vixen, and fond of law. Now would you believe what I'm going to till you? he tould me of his honour—

MR CARVER
Of me, his patron?

CATTY
Of you, his patron, sir. He tould me your honour—which is a slander, as we all here can witness, can't we? by his honour's contempt of Pat Coxe—yet O'Blaney said you was as fond and proud of having informers about you as a rat-catcher is of rats.

MR CARVER
Mistress Catherine Rooney, and all you good people,—there is a great deal of difference between obtaining information and encouraging common informers.

CATTY
There is, I'm sinsible.
[Aside to her **SON**]
Then he's a good magistrate—except a little pompous, mighty good.
[Aloud to **MR CARVER**]
Then I beg your honour's pardon for my bad behaviour, and bad language and all. 'Twas O'Blaney's fau't—but he's down, and don't trample on the fallen.

OLD McBRIDE
Don't defind O'Blaney! Oh! the villain, to rob me of all my hard arnings. Mrs. Catty, I thank you as much as a heavy heart can, for you're ginerous; and you, Randal, for your—

RANDAL
Is it for loving her, when I can't help it?—who could?

OLD McBRIDE [Sighing deeply]
But still it goes against the father's heart to see his child, his pride, go pinnyless out of his house.

PHIL
Then, sir, father dear, I have to tell you she is not pennyless.—But I would not tell you before, that Randal, and Catty too, might show themselves what they are. Honor is not pennyless: the three hundred you gave me to lodge with O'Blaney is safe here.
[Opening his pocket-book]
—When I was going to him with it as you ordered, by great luck, I was stopped by this very quarrel and riot in Ballynavogue:—he was the original cause of kicking up the riot, and was summoned before your honour,—and here's the money.

OLD McBRIDE
Oh, she's not pinnyless! Well, I never saw money with so much pleasure, in all my long days, nor could I think I'd ever live to give it away with half so much satisfaction as this minute. I here give it, Honor, to Randal Rooney and you:—and bless ye, child, with the man of your choice, who is mine now.

MRS CARVER [Aside to **MR CARVER**]
My dear, I wish to invite all these good people to a wedding dinner; but really I am afraid I shall blunder in saying their names—will you prompt me?

MR CARVER
[Aside to **MRS CARVER**]
Why really I am not used to be a prompter; however, I will condescend to prompt you, Mrs. Carver.

[He prompts, while she speaks.

MRS CARVER
Mr. Big Briny of Cloon, Mr. Ulick of Eliogarty, Mr. Charley of Killaspugbrone, and you, Mrs. Catty Rooney, and you, Mr. McBride, senior, and you, Mr. Philip McBride, no longer flourishing Phil; since you are now all reconciled, let me have the pleasure of giving you a reconciliation dinner, at the wedding of Honor McBride, who is an honour to her family, and Randal Rooney, who so well deserves her love.

The **McBRIDES** and **ROONIES** [Joining in the cry]
Long life and great luck to your ladyship, that was always good!

MR CARVER
And you comprehend that I beg that the wedding may be celebrated at Bob's Fort.

ALL [Join in crying]
Long may your honour's honour reign over us in glory at Bob's Fort!

CATTY [Cracking her fingers]
A fig for the bog of Ballynascraw!—Now 'tis all Love and no Law!

Maria Edgeworth – A Short Biography

Maria Edgeworth was born at Black Bourton, Oxfordshire on January 1st 1768, the second child of Richard Lovell Edgeworth and Anna Maria Edgeworth (née Elers).

Her early years were with her mother's family in England. Sadly, her mother died when Maria was only five. When her father married his second wife, Honora Sneyd, in 1773, the family went to live at his estate, Edgeworthstown, in County Longford, Ireland.

Maria was later sent to Mrs. Lattafière's school in Derby after Honora fell ill in 1775. There she studied dancing, French and other subjects. After Honora died in 1780 Maria's father married Honora's sister, Elizabeth, causing much social disapproved.

Maria transferred to Mrs. Devis's school in Upper Wimpole Street, London. Her father began to focus more attention on Maria in 1781 when she nearly lost her sight to an eye infection.

She returned home to Ireland at 14, and took charge of her younger siblings. She herself was home-tutored by her father in Irish economics and politics, science, literature and law. Despite her youth literature was in her blood.

She became her father's assistant in managing the Edgeworthstown estate, which had become run-down during the family's absence. Maria would now live and write there for the rest of her life.

With her father she began a lifelong academic collaboration. She meticulously detailed daily Irish life; a valuable lodestone of references for later use in her novels. Maria mixed with the Anglo-Irish gentry, and her aunt, Margaret Ruxton of Blackcastle, supplied her with the novels of Anne Radcliffe and William Godwin and encouraged her ambition to write.

Edgeworth's first published work in 1795 was 'Letters for Literary Ladies'. That same year 'An Essay on the Noble Science of Self-Justification', written for a female audience, states that the fair sex is endowed with an art of self-justification and women should use their gifts to continually challenge the force and power of men, especially their husbands, with wit and intelligence.

In 1796 her first children's book, 'The Parent's Assistant', which included the much loved short story 'The Purple Jar' was published.

In 1798 her father married for the fourth and last time, this time to Frances Beaufort. Frances was a year younger than Maria and they quickly became close.

'Practical Education' (1798) is a progressive work on education that combines the ideas of Locke and Rousseau with scientific inquiry. Edgeworth believed that "learning should be a positive experience and that the discipline of education is more important during the formative years than the acquisition of knowledge." The ultimate goal of Edgeworth's system was to create an independent thinker who understands the consequences of his or her actions.

Her first novel, 'Castle Rackrent' (1800) was published anonymously without her father's knowledge. It was an immediate success and firmly established Maria's appeal to the public.

'Belinda' (1801), was her first full-length novel. It dealt with love, courtship, and marriage, and she examined these as conflicts within her "own personality and environment; conflicts between reason and feeling, restraint and individual freedom, and society and free spirit." Startlingly, 'Belinda' also included a depiction of interracial marriage between an African servant and an English farm-girl. Later editions of the novel, in line with unforgiving times, removed these sections.

Frances also pushed the family to travel more first London (1800), the Midlands (1802) and later the continent; first to Brussels and then to France. They met all the notables, with Maria even receiving a proposal of marriage from a Swedish courtier.

'Tales of Fashionable Life' (1809 and 1812) is a 2-series collection of short stories that often had its focus on the life of women. The second series was so successful that she was now the most commercially successful novelist of her age and ranked alongside her contemporaries Jane Austen and Sir Walter Scott.

On a visit to London in 1813, she met many notables including Lord Byron. She entered into a long correspondence with Sir Walter Scott after the publication of 'Waverley' in 1814, in which he acknowledged her influence, and they formed a lasting friendship. She visited him in Scotland at Abbotsford House in 1823 and the following year he visited Edgeworthstown.

After debating the issue with the economist David Ricardo, Maria came to believe that better management and the further use of science in agriculture would raise food production and help to lower prices. They were both in favour of Catholic Emancipation, enfranchisement for Catholics without property restrictions, agricultural reform and increased educational opportunities for women.

She worked particularly hard to improve the living standards of the poor in Edgeworthstown and to provide schools for the local children whatever their denomination.

After her father's death in 1817 she edited his memoirs, and extended them with her biographical addenda. Her father had married 4 times and sired 22 children. At the height of her creative endeavours, Maria had written, "Seriously it was to please my Father I first exerted myself to write, to please him I continued."

Maria worked for the relief of the famine-stricken Irish peasants during the Irish Potato Famine. She wrote 'Orlandino' and gave the proceeds to the Relieve Fund. However, during the famine her 'business head' insisted that only those tenants who had paid their full rent would receive any relief. She also punished any tenants who voted against her Tory preferences.

'Helen' (1834) is Maria Edgeworth's final novel, the only one she wrote after her father's death. Here the focus was on characters and situation and not moral lessons.

William Rowan Hamilton was elected president of the Royal Irish Academy and Maria's advice was constantly sought especially regarding literature in Ireland. She suggested that women should be allowed to participate in Academy events. Hamilton made Maria an honorary member in 1837.

After a visit to see her relations Maria was struck with severe chest pains and died suddenly of a heart attack in Edgeworthstown on 22nd May 1849. She was 81.

Maria Edgeworth is buried in the family tomb at St. John's Church, Edgeworthstown, Longford, Ireland.

Maria Edgeworth – A Concise Bibliography

Letters for Literary Ladies (1795) Second Edition (1798)
An Essay on the Noble Science of Self-Justification (1795)
The Parent's Assistant (1796)
Practical Education (1798) (2 Vols; collaborated with her father and step-mother)
Castle Rackrent (1800) Novel
Early Lessons (1801)
Moral Tales (1801)
Belinda (1801) Novel
The Mental Thermometer (1801)
Essay on Irish Bulls (1802)
Popular Tales (1804)
The Modern Griselda (1804)
Moral Tales for Young People (1805) (6 Vols)
Leonora (1806)
Essays in Professional Education (1809)
Tales of Fashionable Life (1809)

Ennui (1809) Novel
The Absentee (1812) Novel
Patronage (1814) Novel
Harrington (1817) Novel
Ormond (1817) Novel
Comic Dramas (1817)
Memoirs of Richard Lovell Edgeworth (1820) Editor
Rosamond: A Sequel to Early Lessons (1821)
Frank: A Sequel to Frank in Early Lessons (1822)
Tomorrow (1823) Novel
Helen (1834) novel
Orlandino (1848) Temperance novel